Geo. B. Loring

Proceedings of a National Convention of Cattle Breeders and others

Geo. B. Loring

Proceedings of a National Convention of Cattle Breeders and others

ISBN/EAN: 9783337146580

Printed in Europe, USA, Canada, Australia, Japan

Cover: Foto ©ninafisch / pixelio.de

More available books at **www.hansebooks.com**

PROCEEDINGS

OF A

NATIONAL CONVENTION

OF

CATTLE BREEDERS AND OTHERS

CALLED IN

CHICAGO, ILLINOIS, NOVEMBER 15 AND 16, 1883,

BY THE

HON. GEO. B. LORING,

COMMISSIONER OF AGRICULTURE,

TO CONSIDER THE SUBJECT OF

CONTAGIOUS DISEASES OF DOMESTIC ANIMALS.

WASHINGTON:
GOVERNMENT PRINTING OFFICE.
1883.

PROCEEDINGS OF THE CONVENTION.

In September last the Commissioner of Agriculture of the United States issued the following circular call:

UNITED STATES DEPARTMENT OF AGRICULTURE,
Washington, D. C., September 21, 1883.

A convention of representatives of all classes interested in the animal industries of the United States will be held in Chicago, Thursday and Friday, November 15 and 16, 1883, for conference concerning contagious diseases among our domestic animals.

In addition to addresses and reports, the following topics are proposed for discussion.

1. The extent to which contagious diseases exist among domestic animals in this country.

2. The modes by which they are introduced or disseminated.

3. Methods by which they may be eradicated or infected districts be isolated.

4. The efficiency of existing legislation relative to such diseases.

It is desired that this convention may be national and thoroughly representative in its character. The time and place have been selected for the convenience of the large number of those directly interested in the questions to be discussed, who are expected to be in attendance at the Annual Fat Stock Show under the auspices of the Illinois State Board of Agriculture, and meetings of a number of important live stock associations to be held during the continuance of this show.

Agricultural, live stock, and dairy associations are invited to send representatives, and all persons interested in breeding, rearing, transporting, importing, or exporting any class of farm animals will be welcomed to the convention.

GEO. B. LORING,
Commissioner of Agriculture.

Pursuant to the place and date mentioned, the several delegates met and were called to order by Prof. G. E. Morrow, of the Illinois State University, at Champaign, Ill. He said:

GENTLEMEN: You are all aware that we meet as a National Convention of those interested in the animal industries of the country, at the call of the Commissioner of Agriculture, Dr. Loring, at whose request I have the honor to call you to order. I hold in my hand a letter from Dr. Loring explaining his enforced absence from this meeting, and I know that each and every one present shares with me the deep regret I feel because of his absence. I know how thoroughly sincere Dr. Loring's words of regret are, and no one feels it more than we do. It was manifestly fitting that this call should proceed from a national source, thus removing it from any possible suspicion that it was from any one class or any one section. I can assure you that it is the earnest wish of Dr. Loring that this Convention shall be thoroughly repre-

3

sentative, and I am glad to see before me quite a number of familiar faces, and whose names will be a sufficient guarantee of the successful outcome of our deliberations. In order, therefore, that we may be able to effect an organization, I suggest that the roll of States be called and that the list of delegates be reported at once. With the understanding that it is Dr. Loring's desire that every gentleman interested directly in any branch of the animal industry shall be free to a voice in the proceedings of the meeting, the call of States will now be made.

Mr. J. H. SANDERS, of Illinois. I suggest, Mr. Chairman, that gentlemen present, without waiting for a formal call of States. hand in their list on slips of paper or any other convenient form, and then we can proceed to a temporary organization.

Professor McMURTRIE, of Illinois. I don't like to interpose a suggestion thus early in the proceedings. but I think it would be a good idea for the States to be called and some member of the delegation could then hand in his list for entry and classification.

The chairman then called the roll of States and Territories, and the following list of 175 delegates. representing 20 States and Territories, was reported and enrolled :

Alabama—J. D. McFarland.

Arizona—J. G. Gosper.

Colorado—W. J. Wilson, H. T. Metcalf, G. W. Rusk, Carey Culver, —— Culver, —— Maxwell.

District of Columbia—Dr. D. E. Salmon.

Illinois—G. W. Curtis. J. K. Shaver, J. M. Thompson, D. N. Foster, J. M. Chambers, J. H. Sanders, D. W. Smith, J. R. Scott, A. B. Hostetter, J. H. Pickrell, C. M. Culbertson, Prof. G. E. Morrow.

Iowa—L. S. Coffin, W. R. Matthew, James Morgan, D. M. Mouinger. H. C. Wheeler, Fitch B. Stacy, Hon. J. B. Grinnell. Hon. John Scott, Thomas B. Wales, R. D. Kellogg, W. R. Nugent, M. L. Dwin. J. Clark. D. Bonnett, George Chase. H. B. Griffin, Joseph Sproat, C. R. Smith, B. H. Taylor, W. T. Smith, E. F. Brockway. J. R. Shaffer. J. J. Snouffer, L. C. Baldwin, R. C. Webb, J. D. Brown.

Kentucky—Hon. J. S. Williams, James Chorn, B. A. Tracy, C. Thompson, C. Estell, B. F. Vanmeter, J. C. Hamilton, George Hamilton, C. R. Esten, W. W. Estell, W. W. Hamilton, A. W. Hamilton, D. A. Gay, W. Yarr. A. C. Bean, W. Garner, C. Scott, R. Owen, G. Hill, T. C. Anderson, C. Howell, W. Points, J. Kendall.

Minnesota—George E. Case.

Maryland—Edward B. Emory.

Massachusetts—Prof. L. S. Thayer.

Michigan—I. H. Butterfield, jr., William Ball, E. R. Phillips, —— Sweet, A. J. Murray, Prof. E. A. A. Grange, C. F. Moore, R. A. Remick, Edwin Phelps, R. B. Caruss.

Missouri—S. E. Ward.

New York—T. G. Yeomans, Prof. James Law, Col. F. D. Curtis,

E. A. Powell, Joseph Harris, G. S. Miller, W. C. Brayton, Prof. J. P. Roberts, —— Wing.

Nebraska—Prof. S. R. Thompson, O. M. Douse, Watson Pickrell, Hon. William Dailey, P. Winslow.

New Jersey—John Crane.

Ohio—W. N. Cowden, L. B. Harris, W. I. Chamberlain, James W. Fleming, J. C. Levering, W. S. Foster, J. H. Brigham, L. N. Bonham, Leo Weltz, Frank Fleming, John Gould, M. J. Lawrence, Calvin Dodge, S. H. Todd, D. W. Todd, William Alwood, —— Lemmust, W. R. Parsons, Z. E. Shook, O. E. Niles, Prof. —— Niles, Prof. I. V. Newton, I. S. Robinson, W. S. Delatast, M. P. Steddon, Prof. T. B. Cotton, J. Corwin, R. C. Skinner.

Pennsylvania—Edgar Huidekoper, J. C. Thornton, Julius LeMoyne, James L. Henderson, W. B. McKerrnan, Prof. John W. Gadsden, James B. Wilson, Samuel P. Fergus, W. M. Dinsmore, J. H. Clark, P. G. Walker, J. G. Paxton, J. M. Thompson.

Tennessee—W. P. Johnson, J. E. Wilcox, M. S. Cockrill, John Overton.

Texas—George B. Loving.

Wisconsin—Prof. —— Henry, Hon. Hiram Smith.

Wyoming—Hon. J. M. Carey, Hon. Thomas Sturgis, Hon. W. C. Irvine, Hon. H. E. Teschemacher, Hon. A. H. Swan, J. H. Pratt, John Clay, May Goldschmidt, John Hunton, S. H. Hardin, W. H. Parker, R. A. Torrey, G. Holden, —— Stevens, George Morgan, Prof. James D. Hopkins.

West Virginia—J. M. Kirk, L. P. Sisson, T. R. Carskaden, T. H. Buchanan, I. B. Carskaden, C. P. Waugh, O. A. Lewis, O. M. Kirk, Obed Bath, Aaron Baker.

Mr. STURGIS, of Wyoming. Gentlemen of the Convention, in the absence of Dr. Loring I propose to you as your temporary chairman, Professor Morrow. I move that he be made temporary chairman.

The motion was agreed to.

Professor MORROW, of Illinois. I thank you heartily for this honor, for I count it an honor to preside, even temporarily, over so important a meeting. There are many things I should be glad to say, but I shall try to set an example by not occupying the time of the Convention in saying fancy things.

Mr. GOSPER, of Arizona. I move the appointment of Mr. Sturgis of Wyoming, as temporary secretary.

Mr. STURGIS. I appreciate the gentleman's consideration, but I shall be unable to act, as I have duties in connection with my own delegation.

The Hon. L. S. Coffin. of Iowa, was thereupon nominated and elected temporary secretary.

The CHAIRMAN. Now, to expedite matters, though I leave it entirely in the hands of the Convention, I will suggest that a committee on permanent organization be appointed, to consist of one member from each State and Territory represented.

A DELEGATE. I move that the plan suggested be adopted.

The motion was agreed to, and upon call the following named gentlemen were selected to represent their respective States upon the committee:

Alabama, J. D. McFarland; Colorado, W. J. Wilson; District of Columbia. Dr. D. E. Salmon; Illinois, John R. Scott; Iowa, W. T. Smith; Kentucky, James Chorn; Maryland, Edward B. Emory; Massachusetts, Prof. L. S. Thayer; Michigan, I. H. Butterfield, jr.; Missouri, Col. S. E. Ward; Nebraska, Prof. S. R. Thompson; New York, Prof. James Law; Ohio, W. N. Cowden; Pennsylvania, J. C. Thornton; Tennessee, J. E. Wilcox; West Virginia, T. R. Carskaden; Wisconsin, Hon. Hiram Smith; Wyoming, Hon. J. M. Carey.

The CHAIRMAN. I will suggest that this committee retire and present a report as soon as possible. I would call the attention of the Convention to the fact that we have with us this morning two gentlemen from Canada. I think it would be well to have their names enrolled, but under a strict construction of the call the Chair would not be at liberty to do so.

A DELEGATE. I move that the provinces of Canada be called.

The motion was agreed to, and upon call Hon. M. H. Cockran responded from the province of Quebec, and Prof. Simon Beatty from the province of Ontario.

The CHAIRMAN. I will take the liberty of nominating the Hon. W. T. Smith, of Iowa, as the chairman of the committee on permanent organization, at least until the committee takes further action.

Hon. J. S. WILLIAMS, of Kentucky. I wish to make one suggestion. It strikes me as almost impossible to get a large attendance in the daytime of the stock men of the country. The fat-stock show is to be held here, beginning to-day and extending up to next Tuesday or Wednesday. There are engaged and interested in this exhibition three hundred or four hundred men—the very men we wish to meet—and but a small number of them can be here in the day-time. I want to ask if it will not be better, all things considered, to hold our meetings in the evening. Now, for instance, I see around me several who want to go to the sale of cattle this afternoon, and then there are other of these sales to-morrow and next day, and so on extending up to as late as next Wednesday, and the fat-stock show is going on all the time. Will it not be best for us to have our meetings in the evening? We certainly could get a much larger attendance.

Mr. THOMPSON, of Kentucky. I hope an organization will be made first, and then this matter can be considered.

Mr. WILLIAMS. I merely mentioned it now because it may be the intention to have a report made immediately.

The CHAIRMAN. The Chair will say that he fully appreciates the force of the remarks made by the gentleman from Kentucky [Mr. Williams], but this evening other important meetings are to be held. The American Hereford Association have a meeting, as do also two agricultural associations in the interest of the horse, not quite so directly connected with the specific object of this Convention perhaps, but there are some who would like to be present at some one of these meetings. Without wishing at all to dictate the action of the Convention I will suggest, with Mr. Thompson, that it will be well for us first to get our work somewhat in hand and started.

Mr. J. H. SANDERS, of Illinois. If you will indulge me a word in relation to this matter, I will say that there are two other organizations now meeting here, the sheep breeders and swine breeders. I presume after to-night the rush of these public meetings will be over, for this room at least, and I beg that this Convention will not ·attempt to rush its proceedings. I hope that it will proceed calmly and deliberately, and take time to thoroughly digest every step that shall be taken with care and due consideration. I do think it is impracticable at night to get a large proportion of these representative men at a meeting. They are all interested in some special meeting to be held to-night. These meetings were called a year ago—most of them—and it is impossible to make changes. I really think we should take ample time to digest every step that is taken.

The CHAIRMAN. Gentlemen, if you will pardon me, and I know you will, I have at my right a gentleman who is interested in agriculture in the State and nation, and I have taken the liberty in advance of inviting Governor Hamilton, of the State of Illinois, in which we meet to-day, to say a fews words to you. [Applause.]

Governor HAMILTON. Mr. Chairman and gentlemen of the Convention : When I accepted the very kind and very urgent invitation of Professor Morrow and others to meet with you this morning for a short time, it was with the distinct understanding that I was not expected to deliver an address. I am very happy, however, to have the privilege of meeting, for a necessarily short time, inasmuch as my official duties call me this evening back to the capital, such a fine representative body of men—as fine in appearance and in general cast as a representative body of men can be in any direction or interest—as fully up to the standard of development and of good appearance in the line of animals called men as is the gathering over here in the Exposition Building in the line of animals called fat stock. [Applause.] I am most sincerely sorry, gentlemen, with all of you no doubt, that Dr. Loring is not present, for I have anticipated for some time the pleasure of listening to that distinguished gentleman.

I fully appreciate the importance of this conference, and of the objects of this Convention, as I understand them, to consider the subject of contagious diseases among animals, their cause, their ravages, and means of prevention and cure. We, in this State, are especially interested in this matter. Since it has been my privilege to preside as chief executive of the State of Illinois we have had considerable trouble in that direction among our stock raisers. During the session of the last legislature, last winter and spring, it became apparent that something must be done by the State government, and by legislative action, to prevent so far as possible the spread of the deadly disease known to stockmen as glanders among horses, which had made its appearance in some parts of the State. It happened that at that time we had upon the statute-books of Illinois an act providing for the prevention and suppression of pleuro-pneumonia among cattle, under which act a State veterinarian was provided, and also a fund to be used by him in connection with his work. That fund, I am happy to say, however, it was unnecessary to use, at least any great portion of it, as the disease, pleuro-pneumonia, did not make its appearance. That act was amended last winter so as to include measures for meeting the ravages of the disease called "glanders," which, as I said before, began to break out, as the Irishman said, "In spots here and there," but in a great many spots, and I have found out that the probabilities are that if it had not been for prompt legislative action we should have suffered to a very much greater extent than we have. The State veterinary surgeon, under my direction, has been very busy during the summer and fall in performing his duties under that act. He has discovered a great many cases, and I doubt not has stopped, to a large extent, the ravages of the disease. The act provides that after a visit and examination by the State veterinarian the animal, if affected, may be condemned, or sequestered, or quarantined, as he may direct, and with these facilities, in connection with certain local facilities and veterinary surgeons, if it is found that the animal is afflicted he may condemn it and have it destroyed, the State paying the amount of the assessment. The law has worked to the very great advantage of the State, and apparently with little friction. If other contagious diseases could be similarly dealt with either through the action of State government, or even of the National Government, by appropriations for carrying out the provisions of law, it would be of very great value to the animal industry of the States and of the United States.

There is an affliction among swine which still exists to some extent, not only in this but other Western States. In this State it has not been very destructive, but if some measures could be agreed upon, or discovered by somebody to stop the ravages of that disease it would certainly save thousands if not millions of dollars to the stock raisers of the West. It seems to me there ought to be no difficulty since the experience we have had in this matter. About six years ago, while I was a member of the senate of this State, a gentleman proposed by way of a bill a very large reward to any one who should discover an unfailing remedy for hog cholera. It was simply proposed and mentioned in the newspapers. It was not passed into law and no further action was taken upon it, and now I receive on an average five letters a week asking for the particulars of that reward and if there is still any way to get the money. I am sure that in this Convention, composed as it is of gentlemen of scientific attainment, and stockmen, and those skilled in veterinary surgery and other matters connected with stock raising, some practical action will be taken which I trust will result in the enactment of some wholesome law under the operation of which our interests will be protected. I have been intensely interested in this matter, not only as chief executive, but in the operations of farming in this State. I have not come here for the purpose of delivering an address, for I have prepared none, and as I have said before none was expected from me; but I welcome you most heartily to the State of Illinois, in which your Convention called for so important a purpose meets to-day, and I bespeak for you abundant success in your efforts to secure for your interests all proper legislation. Thanking you for your attention, I bid you good day. [Applause.]

The CHAIRMAN. I would suggest that we now appoint a committee on order of business. I simply suggest this and leave it entirely in the hands of the Convention.

Mr. SMITH, of Iowa. I move that the Chair appoint a committee of five on order of business.

Mr. STURGIS, of Wyoming. I would like to ask the gentleman whether, in his motion for a committee on order of business, he contemplates the appointment of a committee to discuss the subjects that may come before the Convention, or is it simply to define the order of the questions to be discussed, or is there some other business which requires to have a routine arrangement.

The CHAIRMAN. The thought of the Chair was this: That at any such meeting there are many questions which come up, and there are many gentlemen who have important suggestions to make, and if all these could be reported to this committee, it would be competent for them to report what, in their judgment, should come before the Convention, but of course subject to the action of the Convention.

Mr. C. E. SMITH, of Iowa. I had in view that this committee, being small and not unwieldy, could report the order of procedure of the Convention, recommend time, and so forth.

The motion was agreed to; and the chairman appointed on the committee, Messrs. C. E. Smith, of Iowa, Pickrell, of Illinois, Murray, of Detroit, Mich., Chamberlain, of Ohio, and Van Meter, of Kentucky.

Mr. GRINNELL, of Iowa. Mr. Chairman, I would make this suggestion, that as we have come together as stock raisers from all parts of the country, that we hear from gentlemen who have these afflictions that we have come here to seek remedy for; whether it is glanders or hog cholera, or anything of the kind—not an agreeable matter, it is true, but, sir, I am not advised as an agriculturist in regard to the prevalence of this disease that we have come here to combat. If any man has any trouble, not in his own immediate family [laughter], but in his neighborhood, I think it is a good time to speak out and talk about it. We come here to learn and to sympathize if necessary. There is here a gentleman from the plains, and I refer to him because he happens to come from the State of Iowa—a Mr. Swan. I suppose that his herd numbers about 49,000, and I should like to know if there is any Texas fever among them, and if there are other gentlemen who can give us information on this subject I should like to hear from them.

The CHAIRMAN. One moment. The Chair desires to say that he is informed that Mr. John Dunn, the British vice-consul, is present at the request of the British Government to attend this Convention. I think perhaps it will be the desire of the Convention to tender him its courtesy and grant him the privilege of a seat with us.

Mr. SANDERS, of Illinois. The chair can do that without a formal motion.

The CHAIRMAN. Unless there be objection, the gentleman will be invited to a seat with us. The chair will state that Dr. Salmon, the veterinarian of the Department of Agriculture, and who has been directed by Commissioner Loring to prepare a paper representing the information now in possession of the Department upon this subject, is present. I think it will be proper to have that paper early in the proceedings of the Convention. I await the pleasure of the Convention.

Mr. YEOMANS, of New York. I would suggest that if there are other gentlemen who have been invited to address this meeting that there is now an opportunity until this committee are ready to report the subjects that are to be discussed and the order in which they be discussed.

The CHAIRMAN. Doubtless the members of the Convention have read at different times the call for this meeting. We meet as a body composed of all those interested in the cattle and other animal industries of the country. The Commissioner has left it free for the Convention to do what in its wisdom seems to be best; but he suggested in the original call certain topics as especially desirable, in his opinion, to be discussed.

The topics as set forth in the original call were then read.

Mr. KELLOGG, of Iowa. I was much pleased with the suggestion made by the Hon. Mr. Grinnell, and hoped to have heard a response reporting any disease of stock existing in any locality. Before he took his seat he called upon my friend Mr. Swan. There being no response from any gentleman present, the thought occurred to me whether this Convention was not, in a measure, crying fire when there is no blaze. I apprehend, sir, that it is possible that a call for such a Convention as this going out broadcast over the country and across the waters may effect a greater injury than any benefit we may derive from it. I question no man's motive, but I call upon gentlemen present to say if it is not true that any disease whatever among our stock is the exception and not the rule, and I suggest whether it will not be wisdom on our part to be cautious and not create an undue alarm that there are contagious diseases ravaging our country from one end to the other. If we are to establish that fact what will be the result in the sale of our meats? I presume that there may have been some action taken by foreign Governments inimical to the meat growers of this country, in the interest of their own product. That is all right. Nations look out for themselves as well as individuals; but now the cry of "hog cholera" has worn itself out and it is about as hard to find as the milk sickness. You can find hundreds of people to-day who will guarantee to cure your hogs for ten cents each, and will guarantee to give you a dollar a pound for each one that is lost. It is a fact within the scope of my own observation that that disease prevails to a much more limited extent, since farmers have come to get along better in the world, and have arranged their yards more in accordance with hygienic laws, and introduced purer water, and provided better in other ways for their stock. [Applause.] Farmers have come to know that a little common sense relieves them of most of this trouble, and in our western world, from here west, I know of no such thing as contagion among stock, unless it be glanders among horses, and generally when horses get that it is be. cause they have breathed so long that they cannot breathe any longer. [Laughter.] I throw these remarks out as a suggestion. We should not magnify this matter of stock disease to our own detriment.

Mr. PARSONS, of Ohio. It has been my privilege to travel largely this past year among the cattle-raising districts of our country. My observation has been in my personal interest, and I have not found a herd where pleuro-pneumonia existed. I have traveled through the New England States, through New York and Pennsylvania. I learned that there was something like disease in Maryland, and that there had been a sprinkling of it in Pennsylvania; but westward in every direction there is not a shadow nor a semblance of it; there is one fact, however, among weaklings in calves; when the first cold weather struck some herds there was cold upon the lungs and some of those weaklings died, and some of those who have become frightened at this have scattered the news over the country that this was pleuro-pneumonia. It is just the same as a man taking a severe cold and having pneumonia, if neglected. But so far as any contagious disease of this or any other character is concerned, I have not known of a single case in all my travels.

Professor PRENTICE, of Illinois. I would like to say a few words on this subject. I have been eleven years connected with the State University of Illinois, and I can indorse what the gentleman has just said about bronchial pneumonia among calves, and I am certain that men who are not experienced would pronounce that to be contagious pleuro-pneumonia; but such is not the case.

Mr. KELLOGG. I would like to ask the gentleman before he takes his seat, if he has ever known of a case of contagious pleuro-pneumonia in this country?

Professor PRENTICE. Never, sir. I have seen plenty of it in England.

Mr. CLARK, of Iowa. Mr. Chairman, as a stock raiser since 1840, in Iowa, and as a citizen and farmer of that State, having mingled among the stockmen and stock farmers, buying, selling, and raising, I have yet to learn of a man of experience in raising and breeding stock in our State who has yet known the time himself when it was dangerous to go to any other herd in the State of Iowa to purchase stock for his purposes because there was contagious diseases among them. I have handled several thousand head of stock myself. I have wintered them, brought them from the different places west of Iowa, and from Illinois, to my farm, placed them together, cared for them from a year to two years, fattened them and brought them back to this market, and no animal has had a disease which was communicated to it by any other animal. Yet I have been in England and have seen cattle from my State, and some from my own neighborhood, placed at a disadvantage of from $5 to $10 a hundred because of the sanitary regulations which barred out our stock from being shipped through Great Britain, and all because of the fears that have been built up that our stock was diseased. I am glad to know that there is a gentleman representing that country on this floor, and in his hearing I assert, as a stock raiser of Iowa, that the time has never been in Iowa when it was dangerous to bring stock from Illinois, Wisconsin, Michigan, Wyoming, or Utah for fear it would communicate disease. [Applause.]

Mr. COFFIN, of Iowa. I heartily agree with every word that has been said in regard to any contagious disease prevailing at present in these Western States. There is no question about it so far as the cattle disease, pleuro-pneumonia, is concerned; but for fear that this Convention shall be turned aside from the great point that I am so anxious it should meet, I feel called upon to reply to some of the remarks which have been just made. We rejoice and we feel like being grateful, and are grateful, that we have none of this contagious disease in the West; but we must acknowledge and own that we are not without danger. [Applause.] So long as contagious disease exists anywhere in this nation just so long are we in danger, and the object of this Convention is to plan some way and some method to eradicate every vestige of ease from our land. [Renewed applause.] My friend, Hon. Justice Clark, admits that we are discriminated against. Every shipper of a steer from here to England has to suffer a loss of from $10 to $20 from the very fact that there does exist somewhere in this nation a contagious disease, and we are meeting to devise some plan, some method, to remove the cause of that discrimination. [Applause.] Every man in this Convention who is intelligent enough to know anything knows that there exists along our eastern coast this pleuro-pneumonia. We cannot shut our eyes to that; and our steers going from the West have to pass through the Atlantic States. Our English cousins know this fact, and no steer can go from the West through Baltimore, New York, or Philadelphia without being more or less in danger of contagion. [Applause.] Then again we are receiving now very largely breeding stock from the other country. Those cattle have to come through those ports, and I say it is a miracle of good luck that we never have had this disease brought into the West by that means. Now, shall we shut our eyes to the danger that is before us? We don't attempt to tell the world that we have this disease here in the West, and if we did we should tell a falsehood. What we are doing is the planning of measures to prevent and rid ourselves of a danger that we cannot shut our eyes to. [Applause.]

Mr. CLARK, of Iowa. I agree with Mr. Coffin that this Convention should do everything in its power in this direction. What I desired to show was that we have none of this disease in the Western States. I am ready to join any gentleman present in making any arrangement to bring to the attention of Congress the dangers that surround us in order, if possible, that we may prevent this disease from being brought here and continue to be clear of it.

Dr. GADSDEN. I will not take up your time but a moment. What I desire to say is that England does not want any information from this Convention as to where contagious diseases exist in this country. I can assure you that they know where it is as well as we do. Every month they publish in a journal the exact location of all herds that are affected. They know full well that the West has never yet seen this disease. I make this suggestion in order to show that you need not trouble yourselves about England's information on this subject. Where they get it or who informs them I don't know. I was in England last year and I saw there copies of letters and reports from the Agricultural and Treasury Departments—all the information apparently that is in their possession. They know it all, gentlemen, and officially, too.

Mr. Smith, from the committee on permanent organization, presented the following report, which was unanimously agreed to:

President—Hon. John S. Williams, of Kentucky.

Vice-Presidents—Prof. George E. Morrow, of Illinois; Hon. Alfred Batters, of Colorado; Edward A. Powell, of New York; Hon. M. H. Cochrane, of Dominion of Canada.

Secretary—Hon. Thomas Sturgis, of Wyoming.

Assistant Secretary—Edward B. Emory, of Maryland.

The newly-elected president of the Convention was thereupon conducted to the chair, and Professor Morrow said:

GENTLEMEN OF THE CONVENTION: I have the honor to introduce to you a gentleman who is widely known as one largely interested in agriculture and the subjects you are to discuss, and also for his public service in their behalf. [Applause.]

The PRESIDENT: Gentlemen of the Convention, I feel profoundly

grateful to you for this very unexpected honor. I am here rather by
accident than otherwise, but glad of an opportunity of meeting representative men from every section of our country, who are gathered together at this time to consider one of the most vital interests of the
whole people of our land. I cannot, in accepting the honor and respon-
sibilities of presiding over your deliberations, refrain from expressing
my profound regret that the distinguished gentleman whom we all expected to preside over this Convention, the Commissioner of Agriculture, Dr. Loring, is detained at home by sickness. I know that he would
have been able to instruct us upon the subjects that we have met to consider. I came here merely to learn, and not to instruct; for while there
is not a more zealous man in this broad land in the advocacy of measures for your benefit, I am not in possession of information to instruct
you. I have zeal but not knowledge. I have struggled in the Congress
of the United States for years to procure some remedial legislation from
the National Government that might reach the root of the evil.
Perhaps I do not understand the full scope and objects of this meeting; but if I do understand them it is to attempt to procure measures
for the interdiction of foreign and exotic diseases, especially of the
cattle of the country. We do know that certain highly contagious diseases have been imported here from foreign countries,
and have been planted in certain sections of our country; and yet
these diseases are restricted within such narrow limits, that it is
entirely possible and practicable for the National Goverment to stamp
them out wherever they are found, and to take measures for the
prevention of their further introduction. I have endeavored for years
to impress this idea upon Congress. I have labored much upon that
subject; and I have found one great difficulty to be that a majority of
your Representatives had not sufficient information upon this subject
and could not be induced to talk as they should have done. If
you want anything done now you must express your determination.
Also provide funds to send your delegation to Washington to pay its
way; not to buy its way, but to pay its way, for they have got to stay
there and lobby the bill through. Every other interest has its lobby
there, and it is useless to talk about doing anything without money.
The bankers, the iron men, the manufacturers, everybody has a lobby
there except the farmers and stock-raisers, and if you expect to get any
legislation in your interest you must adopt the necessary means to accomplish it. [Great laughter.] We represent the greatest interest of
all. The cattle interest alone amounts to $750,000,000 annually—more
than the tobacco; more than the wheat; more than everything else, and
nearly as much as all others combined, but far more than any one interest: for those things which you produce, your corn and your grass,
go into your stock. Animal productions amount to more than all the
other products of the country combined. Well, now, this disease not only
endangers your herds at home, for we know that they are contagious and

incurable, but while they are yet confined to limited districts we feel certain they have not influenced the cattle trade from west to east; but, when it turns the other way, with the growth of the dairy, the production of milk and butter, how then will it be when shipment of improved bulls must be made west. The misfortune of the thing now is that these diseases are located at the very ports of entry from which you export your cattle, and they cast suspicion over everything you send to foreign countries. You want not only the disease exterminated, but you want that suspicion removed. [Applause.] In my judgment there is no power to do that except the almighty arm of the National Government, which is able to appropriate the necessary means. [Applause.] Foreign countries know us as one people only; they do not understand our dual form of government; that we are a great nation composed of independent commonwealths; they regard us only as the American Government, the Government of the United States; and Illinois and Kentucky and Pennsylvania and New York and Maryland and Virginia, do what they may, can never remove the suspicion of the people in the foreign markets of the world that our meats come to them in an unhealthy and unsound condition, and that the American Government takes upon itself the responsibility of giving clean bills of health. What do we lose by this? What might be our exports to foreign countries? Think of it. We are exporting $15,000,000 annually, and about as much of dead meat of the product of cattle, to say nothing about our hogs, and the suspicion that is cast upon your live-stock has excluded your hogs and your pork from Germany and France, and means such restriction upon your live cattle going to England as to amount almost to a prohibition. Suppose we can remove this. Suppose we can satisfy the foreign countries that all our live animals are free from infection. What might be the extent of our exports? I can assure you that in time they would amount to more, much more, than all of our other exports combined. If we had a free market; if you men could send your 1,200 and 1,400 pound bullocks to England, and instruct your continental grazers to put them on their pastures and feed them turnips and rich, succulent grasses, they would soon get over the heat and fever and bruises and sores of that long line of transportation from the extreme West, 1,500 miles by rail and 3,000 miles by sea; they could take them and finish them up and bring them back into the market, and they would bring as high a price as British beef. [Applause.] But as it is they have to be slaughtered in the pens immediately, and if there is a glut in the market at the time your beef is sold at a sacrifice, for they cannot be transported back, nor is there any ice there to preserve the meat, and you lose sometimes from $35 to $40 per head. Remove this taint and instead of shipping from $15,000,000 to $20,000,000 annually of live cattle you would ship from $250,000,000 to $300,000,000. Think of the advantage, you men of the West, if you could ship your 1,300 or 1,400 pound bullocks abroad and have them placed in the shambles there as fresh and

as juicy and pure as the finest they could raise abroad. Instead of getting 3 cents a pound you would get 6 cents for cattle in this market; and
if the market was free, instead of 4 cents for your hogs you would get 7 or
8 cents. This is indeed a mighty question; it is the greatest question
of all that can be presented to the farmers of this country—the question
of exterminating this disease and removing this suspicion [applause],
and we never can prosper until that thing is done. [Renewed applause.]
I shall not attempt to make you a speech. I am here merely to hear
and to see how much help you are going to give me this winter in pro-
curing the adoption of measures for the suppression of these plagues.
I cannot do it alone. You have in your hands the means to influence
your members of Congress—your Senators, and Representatives in the
House—and let me assure you that you have got to bring that influence
to bear upon them, you have got to knock loud and often, before they
will listen to your appeals. [Applause.]

May I ask what is your order of business?

Mr. GOSPER. of Arizona Territory. I simply rise to request the Chairman to ask his secretary to rise and make a bow to the audience, so that
we may be able to recognize him hereafter. [Great laughter.]

Mr. STURGIS, of Wyoming. I don't think that any remarks are necessary from me, Mr. Chairman.

A DELEGATE. Mr. President, I understand that the committee on
order of business is ready to report. Will the chairman of that committee rise and state the facts?

Mr. C. E. SMITH, of Iowa. We have hastily prepared a report, in order
to give the Convention something to work upon, and the secretary will
read the report.

Mr. COFFIN, of Iowa. I am very anxious to hear something from Mr.
Sturgis, because he is one of the prime movers in this movement.

Mr. STURGIS, of Wyoming. Gentlemen, I am less unwilling to say a
few words upon this occasion from the fact that a remark which was made
here this morning seemed to me to furnish a text for your deliberations
to-day which cannot be improved upon. It was said by one of the gentlemen, I think from Iowa, that this disease had never entered his State, and
that he was able to buy cattle from the West without any fear of disease.
Why is it that he says he is able to buy of my friend Mr. Swan without
this fear? It is not because disease has not threatened Wyoming. We
in that Territory take the very deepest interest in this question, and it
arises from the fact that while with you, perhaps, this cattle interest is
one of many industries in your States, with us it is the basis upon which
the entire prosperity of our Territory rests. With us it is the one thing
upon which rests, not only the taxation of the Territory, but the success
of the stores, the manufacturing institutions, the banks, and everything.
With us it is the one thing, and you cannot picture in brighter colors
than we can imagine for ourselves the effect should one of these terrible
bovine scourges invade our Territory. We have been alive to this for

a long time past.   It is no new measure; for we have taken all the means for local protection that our commonwealth can adopt.   Over two years ago a very elaborate bill, combining not only the features of the Illinois law, but also all the best terms of printed legislation on the subject, was passed by our legislature, and under the provisions of that bill we have been locally protected for the past two years.   I will not give you in detail the provisions of that bill.   I will simply say that it provides and makes obligatory on the owner of stock that every bull, every cow, every heifer that he brings into our Territory shall have from our Territorial veterinarian a clean bill of health before he leaves the first station at which he arrives within the Territory.   This you understand is made obligatory.   Our veterinarian has the right not only to detain, to quarantine, but destroy, and the fund for these purposes is received from a special tax.   We have come here as a delegation appointed at a special meeting of our association, and as a member of that delegation I desire to impress upon you the necessity of shutting the stable door before the horse is stolen.   As I say, we have provided at our own doors such measures as we can to prevent the introduction of this disease into our Territory.   Now, we want to prevent the possibility of that disease ever coming to our doors, and to kill it where it now exists. [Applause.] It certainly would be foolish indeed for us to rest in fancied security and be misled into the belief that because we have not had previously much disease that we shall never have it.   There can be no misleading about it, for in a publication of the Commissioner of Agriculture, a copy of which lies before me on the table, it is shown that this disease, especially the scourge of pleuro-pneumonia, exists in at least five of the Atlantic States, and in those States, in a mild form, in not less than two hundred separate localities.   That is not a thing that can be overlooked; it is not a thing that we can say exists there and will never exist anywhere else.   We do believe that at present it is so isolated, and that it is in such localities that, with a moderate expenditure of money by the General Government, directed by careful, scientific, and professional men, it will be possible to eradicate this disease, and if we neglect it we just as earnestly believe that in a few years we shall be in the condition of the British Islands.   The Wyoming delegation, gentlemen, is ready to enter upon the necessary work with time, and labor, and money.   We are in favor of that sort of surgery that cuts off the leg in order to save the life [Applause.]

The PRESIDENT. I understand that the committee on order of business is now ready to report.   The secretary of the committee will read the report.

Mr. Chamberlain, from the committee, then presented the following report:

The committee on order of business beg leave to report that, in order that this Convention may at once proceed to its intended work, we recommend—

First. That we at once listen to papers and addresses from Professor Law and J. H.

7924 C B——2

Sanders, of the Treasury Commission, Dr. D. E. Salmon, of the Agricultural Department and Dr. Jas. D. Hopkins, of Wyoming, stating the present condition of investigation by their commissions and by the Department, and such recommendations as they may see fit to make to this Convention for its action, looking towards effecting necessary legislation.

Second. That the Convention adjourn for dinner at 1 p. m., and hold other meetings at 3.30 and 9 p. m. to-day, and at 8 a. m. to-morrow, or until the objects of the Convention have been attained.

The committee request that persons who have papers or addresses of a practical nature that they are ready to present should state the fact to the committee that it may arrange programme for future meetings to-day and to-morrow.

The committee will meet this morning in this room at the reporter's table to listen to suggestions and receive names of parties that are likely to present papers of real value to the Convention.

Respectfully submitted.

CAREY R. SMITH, Chairman.
W. I. CHAMBERLAIN, Secretary.

A DELEGATE. I move that the report be adopted by sections.

The motion was agreed to.

The first section was thereupon read and adopted.

Upon consideration of the second section the following discussion took place :

Mr. LAWRENCE, of Ohio. It seems to me that half past three is pretty late for our afternoon session.

Mr. CHAMBERLAIN, of Ohio. The reason for the action of the committee was that it was thought that a large part of the audience would wish to be present in other places between the time of adjournment and the hour named.

The PRESIDENT. I think it will be impossible for many to come even at that hour. These sales will be in progress, and I know there are many who wish to attend them. The sale is not only to-day but to-morrow and next day. I merely throw out this suggestion. It strikes me that we might have a morning session at which the committees could report and the routine business be discussed, but by all means let us have a night session. We are considering a very important matter, and we should have a meeting at night when these gentlemen can all be present. We can devote hours to it then, and sit until one o'clock if we choose. All these men are interested in this exhibition and in buying and selling high-bred stock. It is very important to have them with us. Their influence is worth a great deal to us, and I hope some one will move that we have a night session instead.

Mr. W. T. SMITH, of Iowa. I move that when this Convention adjourns it be to meet at seven o'clock this evening.

Mr. CAREY E. SMITH, of Iowa. I would like to say in defense of the action of the committee, that we cannot hold any meeting at any hour that will not affect some one of the many meetings and attractions here. We also recognized the fact that there are gentlemen here who have come thousands of miles for the express purpose of moving in this work.

We cannot put this off from time to time to accommodate this State and that State, therefore we tried to harmonize and hold the evening sessions rather late in order that some of these meetings could get through and their members could attend our meeting.

The second section was then adopted, and, upon motion, the remaining section was adopted.

Mr. GRINNELL, of Iowa. Mr. Chairman, I presume there are at least fifty persons present whom I should be glad to hear from; they are all able men, and some of them scientific gentlemen in the professions. I move, sir, in order that each may have a chance, that gentlemen occupying the time of the Convention be limited to one-half an hour, and we can do as they do in Congress, give them " leave to print " [laughter] unti they have been heard all around.

The PRESIDENT. I would say to the gentleman that some of the gentlemen who are here have been specially called upon to address us, and that the time mentioned would neither be long enough nor fair to them.

Mr. GRINNELL. Well, sir, we can ask them to go on when the time has expired.

The PRESIDENT. In accordance with the recommendation of the committee on order of business, Professor Law's paper is first in order, and I have the pleasure of introducing that gentleman, who will now address you. [Applause.]

Professor Law, of Cornell University, then addressed the Convention. He said:

Mr. PRESIDENT AND GENTLEMEN : No more important question can to-day engage the attention of the citizen or statesman than that of the contagious diseases of animals and the means of suppressing and extinguishing them. This subject has been too long neglected and is liable to continued neglect, for the reason that those who suffer pecuniarily from these affections have a deep personal interest in keeping the extent and even the very fact of their losses a profound secret. The city milkman who loses from the bovine lung plague in a single half year a number of cows equal to the entire herd that he holds at any one time would drive his customers to other dairies and invoke financial ruin if he published the fact of his heavy losses. The horse dealer would find his stock a drug in the market if he were injudicious enough to report that glandered animals had occupied his stalls. The flockmaster would throw away his chances of a remunerative sale if he let it be known that his sheep suffered from scab, lung-worms, or foot-rot. The swine-breeder might give up all hope of profit if he allowed that his herds were infested with trichinæ or contaminated with swine-plague.

Yet we well know that these are only examples of the animal contagia now existing among us and that threaten the whole of the live-stock industries of this great country.

TEXAS FEVER—GULF-COAST FEVER.

Our entire Southern coast is contaminated with a poison deadly to all bovine animals that have not been inured to it from the earliest dawnings of life, and Dr. Salmon has shown that this poison is steadily advancing northward, and for aught we yet know may one day cast its withering spell over our countless Northern herds as well. This poison is inherent in the soil, and in a suitable field may live and propagate in the earth independently of animal hosts. It is therefore in one sense even more redoubtable than those animal contagia which have little or no viability or power of self-propagation out of the living animal body. Happily for us, as yet this redoubtable poison cannot survive the winter frosts of our Northern States. Its yearly invasions of our Northern pastures in summer and autumn are as yet effectually repelled by the winter's cold, and the disease has to make a fresh start the next year from its perennial home in the sunny South. Whether it can by a slow and gradual advance through the intermediate climates of the Middle States become finally acclimated and fitted for survival in the extreme North is a question that must be settled by carefully conducted experiment, unless, indeed, we elect to pursue our time-honored policy of letting the experiment be wrought out in the natural way, and of ascertaining, mayhap when too late, that our Northern herds are yearly scourged by the plague, and that our Northern pastures have become permanently saturated with the deadly germs. The prevalence of this poison on the whole coast of the Gulf of Mexico and on the islands in the Gulf suggests that it is an indigenous germ generated in some way in that particular soil, and hence we must learn much more than we as yet know of its life-history before we can decide whether it will ever be possible for us to stamp it out. At present we can prevent its yearly summer invasions of the North and its slower but more permanent advances in the Middle States; we can even habituate young animals to its influence so that they may not fall victims to its ravages; but we cannot promise by any known measures to purify the already contaminated Southern States and guarantee them wholesome to cattle brought from without.

TUBERCULOSIS.

Take another prevalent plague—tuberculosis. There can no longer be a shadow of doubt that this is a contagious disease, and I feel that I can no longer rationally doubt that it is caused by the infinitesimal germ, *Bacillus tuberculosis*, recently discovered by Koch. The fact that this scourge is common to man and a large class of domestic and wild animals places it on a height of sanitary importance that forbids us to ignore it or to contemplate it with feelings other than those of dread and apprehension. The vital statistics of New York City show that 29 per cent. of the mortality in its adult male population is from tuberculosis, and our examination of the herds that supply that city with milk reveals the astounding fact that in certain herds tuberculosis affects 20, 30, and, in some cases, even 50 per cent. Nor is this the worst showing that can be adduced. I have seen single herds of 50 and 60 head in the healthy country districts of New York, in which 90 per cent. were the victims of tuberculosis.

Experiment has shown that this disease is propagated not only by direct inoculation, but by the consumption of the tuberculous flesh and milk, and by the inhalation into the lungs of the virulent particles diffused in the atmosphere in water spray. Nor does this complete the list of its channels of infection. I have recently witnessed in the biological laboratories of Europe the artificial cultivation of the tubercle bacillus on the freshly-cut surfaces of fruits and on sterilized bread, as well as on gelatinous preparations, and have seen the brute sufferers from tuberculosis that have been inoculated from these cultivations. In the face of these evidences that we and our animal possessions are liable to contract this fatal malady by the various channels of simple skin abrasions, ingestion with our food, animal and vegetable, and inhalation with our breath, no one will accuse me of underrating the magnitude of the danger, nor of seeking to undervalue any available measure for its restriction. One stands in wonder that in this conclusion of the nineteenth century the subject should still be comparatively unnoticed and untouched by Governments and by their local and national boards of health.

But, great as is the need of sanitation in this field, and strongly as it appeals to the moral sense, as well as to the instincts of self-preservation of the individual and the community, the fact remains that the subject is too gigantic, the cost of restrictive measures too great, and the results promised us are too partial to warrant the expectation that the Government is prepared as yet to effectually grapple with the evil. The infected animals are scattered all over this great continent. They are found at least as abundantly in the herds of the countries adjoining us, and are liable to cross our frontier at any moment. The infection prevails not in one genus of animals only, but among all domesticated animals, especially the ruminants and omnivora. Thus, in men and domestic animals, we would have to inspect and control not less than 190,000,000 individuals scattered over an area of 3,000,000 square miles. But, in addition to all this, wild animals that successfully evade the domination and control of man, suffer equally with the tame. The poison can survive and multiply not only in a living animal medium, but also in dead vegetable matter; and, finally, man himself furnishes so many victims that after we had done everything possible for the extinction of the poison in beast and vegetable, the sacredness of human life would still set a limit to our suppressive measures, and the virus would continue to be perpetuated everywhere in man, and at frequent intervals to be conveyed anew to the brute. Many millions might be spent on this affection to ths great advantage of the community, with the effect of securing what might approximate to a temporary extinction of the active disease in the lower animals, yet, owing to the persisting consumptions among men, there would be no actual diminution of the infected area, and no one part of the country could be said to have been saved from the blighting presence of this disease. Critics would inveigh against the prophylactic measures with far more effect than they now do against the Jennérian vaccination, and, if unsupported by familiar contemporaneous instances in which contagious diseases had been completely extinguished, the sanitarians would find it hard to obtain a continued supply of the sinews of war and to maintain the humanitarian conflict. A failure after such a crusade had been inaugurated would mean a staggering blow to all sanitary legislation, and a serious retarding of the immeasurable boon which through this means may be secured for suffering humanity. Great and ubiquitous as is the evil of animal tuberculosis, I would advise that for the present no veterinary sanitary legislation for its suppression be sought from the national Congress, but that the subject be for a time left in the hands of municipal health officers, physicians, and hygienists; in other words, let the individual and the local community adopt such protective measures as come within their power, or as the exigencies of their particular case may demand. All such isolated action is confessedly very imperfect and comparatively ineffectual, yet it will be of vast benefit, and will prove a stepping-stone to that national control which I trust many now present may live to see, and which should aim at the entire extinction of this bane of civilization.

SWINE-PLAGUE.

Turn to another of our great prevailing animal plagues. The so-called hog cholera or swine plague has become domiciled in all our great pork-raising districts. A few years ago the annual losses were estimated at $20,000,000, a sum which implies at once a decimation of over 50,000,000 swine, and a general prevalence of the disease wherever swine are bred on a large scale. The great area involved in these ravages, and the numbers of contaminated herds and infected premises, would make any effort to stamp out this disease a herculean task. Again, though there is a presumption that this disease once extirpated would be rooted out for good, still we are not yet certain that it does not arise indigenously on our own land, and that after all our labor and outlay we would not still be continually confronted by new centers of infection developed by unwholesome conditions among badly managed herds. It is more than questionable whether Congress would appropriate the means necessary to stamp out this plague and to thoroughly seclude and disinfect all infected premises, and no one can doubt that it would be next to impossible to secure a continuance of such appropriation if the disease persisted in cropping out anew at frequent intervals and at short distances after millions had been expended for its extinction.

OTHER CONTAGIOUS DISEASES OF ANIMALS.

I dare not try your patience by introducing the question of the other contagious diseases of animals, such as glanders, the various forms of anthrax, milk-sickness, diphtheria, actinomycosis, strangles, influenza, mange, and all the numerous and dangerous forms of animal parasitism; suffice it to say that no one of these presents to us the same favorable conditions for a perfect suppression as does the lung plague of cattle, and for none can we promise the same speedy and absolutely permanent extinction.

LUNG PLAGUE AND TEXAS FEVER AS AFFECTING OUR FOREIGN TRADE.

In this connection it is only just to state that Texas fever assumes a special importance in connection with its occasional exportation to Great Britain in beef cattle. It may therefore be made the occasion of the maintenance of the present slaughtering clause, even after we shall have completely stamped out the lung plague. In this as in the case of the lung plague, it is well at once to face the truth. The Texas fever has an average incubation or latency of one month, and even in cases communicated by inoculation this extends to ten days. It stands therefore side by side with lung plague in the impossibility of checking its exportation by the simple expedient of a professional examination at the port of embarkation. It has been the rule for shippers from Boston and New York to have their cattle examined prior to shipment; but this has not prevented the exportation of twenty-six infected cargoes in the course of the present autumn. It is folly to expect anything like absolute protection from a professional examination without detention, in the case of such a disease, and to advocate such a measure is merely to invite discomfiture and discredit. No veterinarian who would be true to himself and his country would advocate such an examination as an effectual safeguard.

The only protection of our Northern herds and export cattle against the contagion of the Gulf-coast fever must be sought in the absolute prohibition of the movement northward of the cattle from infected districts excepting in the depth of winter. This we must one day secure, and if it is possible to obtain from the present Congress a measure which will accomplish this it will be a matter for profound thankfulness. But we need not close our eyes to the fact that the apprehension of such a law on the part of our Southern Representatives, has been a main cause of the defeat of every important measure for the stamping out of our animal contagia. While therefore strongly in favor of a law that will circumscribe the Southern or Gulf-coast fever, I am convinced that it will be highly injudicious to incorporate any such provision in a bill providing for the extinction of the lung plague. To do so is but to invite and insure defeat. Happily the Gulf-coast cattle fever may be ignored for a year or two without fear of its becoming permanent in any of the Northern localities into which it is yearly introduced. Again any measures which we can at present adopt look not to its definite extinction but only to its limitation to its present area. It is, therefore, as preposterous as injurious to continue to combine these two subjects in any future Congressional bills.

SPECIAL URGENCY OF THE LUNG PLAGUE QUESTION.

The lung plague question is a more urgent one in every sense. This disease is an exotic and if extinguished once would only reappear in case of a new importation from an already infected country. Its area of prevalence in the United States is so limited that it could be easily, with perfect certainty and (relatively to our other contagia) quickly and cheaply extirpated. Unlike Texas fever, anthrax, and tuberculosis, it is not propagated in the soil, &c., nor is it capable of indefinite preservation and accidental increase out of the animal body, and therefore it may be easily extinguished. It is unlike the Texas fever in that it is comparatively unaffected by climate or season, and in that it tends to persist in any locality into which it has once been introduced and where susceptible cattle are found. Every day of its existence on our Eastern seaboard threatens our Western herds even to the coast of the Pacific. The infection of the West, the fountain of our cattle trade, means the infection not only of our roaming Western herds, but of all the channels of trade into which these gravitate, of all our stock-yards, of all our Middle and Eastern States and of our exports. Our present yearly losses from this plague are about $3,000,000 ; our losses in case of the extension we are supposing could not be less than $50,000,000 representing at 5 per cent. a capital of $1,000,000,000. Worse than all, such a tax once imposed can never be wiped out, as no land has ever succeeded in stamping out this disease among roaming herds on unfenced grazing grounds. It is this that is to be feared more than anything else, and if we leave the seed of this scourge to propagate itself on our Eastern seaboard this is what will happen to us sooner or later. On every ground, therefore, whether of commercial economy or of financial foresight, of the attainability of the necessary legislation, or of the assurance of the complete and permanent extinction of the malady to be dealt with, it may be safely claimed that lung plague demands the first measure of veterinary sanitary legislation. To neglect it is to woo a ruinous and irretrievable loss which must forever after bear an invariable relation to our growing herds, and with their increase would ere long reach $100,000,000 in place of $50,000,000 per annum. The restriction of any one of our other animal plagues may be postponed without the overshadowing dangers that threaten from the neglect of this, and no one of these plagues gives the same assurance of a complete and early extinction of the poison under the application of proper methods. To handicap any bill for the extinction of this disease with provisions for any other affection, I cannot but consider as ruinous to the cause, not of anti-lung plague legislation only, but of all veterinary sanitary legislation and work.

It is undoubtedly our duty as sanitarians and citizens to do all in our power to secure by legislation and every other available means the suppression of one and all of the animal plagues of which I have been speaking; but as it is impracticable to secure all this at once, as the demand for the whole would infallibly lose us the whole, and as the lung plague is at once the most urgent and the simplest plague to deal with, and that on which we can go to work with the most perfect confidence of a complete success, this should be provided for in a separate bill, which should furnish ample power and means, and should take precedence of all others.

THE LUNG PLAGUE OF AMERICA THE LUNG PLAGUE OF THE OLD WORLD.

But we are reminded that we have in our midst stockmen who deny the existence of the genuine European lung plague in America, and who quote anonymous veterinarians in support of their assertion. I am in no wise disconcerted by this. In company with other sanitarians I had to meet the same assertions a quarter of a century ago, and the tactics now adopted are the same as were followed then. Then as now the agitation was ascribed to the cupidity of the agitators. Then as now the cattle dealers declared the lung plague a myth and quoted the late Professor Dick to the effect that it was only an inflammation of the lungs caused by impure air. The same professor denied the inoculability of hydrophobia, described rinderpest as a mere impaction of the manifolds, and wrote an article to prove the non-contagiousness of epidemic diseases in general. We all know that personal interest and the love of notoriety will prompt certain men to promulgate dogmas that outrage the intelligence and common sense of the age. There are still, I believe, at Cambridge some learned men who assert that the earth is flat and that the sun revolves around it once in twenty-four hours.

A loss of $500,000,000 from lung plague alone has taught England that she is not dealing with a myth but with a terrible and exacting reality, and a long and most intimate acquaintance with this lung plague has enabled England to pronounce without hesitation on the existence of the same disease in cattle exported from our shores.

To come back to our own case ; our self-appointed judges should have gone to the East and given some attention to the facts of the case before rendering their decision and visiting us with wholesale condemnation. They should have stood with us in the yards of the Blissville distillery in 1879 when the veterinarians who had been hired by Messrs. Gaff, Fleischmann & Co., and who had denounced our work in the public newspapers, and published a certificate that there was not a single case of lung plague in the distillery stables, were invited to select from the cattle we had condemned any that they considered sound, and were furnished in every case, on dissection, with ocular demonstration in the lung extensively and characteristically diseased. They should have stood with us in the field of John E. White, of Sagg, Suffolk County, New York, where nine cattle infected by a bull calf from Brooklyn stood ready to be shot; they should have seen the darkening faces of some scores of the inhabitants, and heard the denunciations and warnings that we would be held personally responsible for what they considered a grave error and a high-handed outrage on property in the slaughter of sound animals. They should have seen the urging necessary to get the executioner to do his duty, and they should have seen the restoration of universal confidence and support when the chests were opened and the masses of loathsome and characteristic disease exposed. They should have accompanied us in the rest of our inspections the same day and heard the men who had been the foremost to denounce us offering to pay out of their own pockets the value of the animals condemned in case they should not be found after death precisely as we had pronounced them. They should have attended us in the whole of our work in the east end of Long Island, and seen that wherever a farmer had taken in a calf out of the infected herd brought from Brooklyn by Billard, there the malady had broken out and decimated the herd. They should have visited with us the fine Jersey herd of Mr. Watrous, Perth Amboy, N. J., where an infected cow brought from a sale in New York City introduced the disease which proved simply ruinous. They should have visited with us the extensive and valuable Jersey herd of Mr. James A. Hoyt, of Patterson, Putnam County, New York, when the introduction of the disease in four cows from New Jersey and Maryland led to the disease of his entire herd and to the loss of upwards of $20,000. They should have witnessed the invasion consequent on the introduction from the Union Stock Yards, New York, of infected animals into the stock farm of Mr. Baldwin, general live stock agent of the Erie Railway, and into the West Chester herd of Mr. Roach, of ship-building fame. They should have investigated the devastations caused in the herd of the Children's Hospital at Willow Brook, Staten Island, through an infected purchase, and of the herd of the Bloomingdale Lunatic Asylum through an infected cow coming to bull. They should have witnessed the thousands of similar cases in New York, New Jersey, Pennsylvania, Delaware, Maryland, and Virginia, and then they would have been in a position to decide justly whether we were dealing with a terribly contagious and fatal disease of the lungs.

I mention these cases of recent infection, not as desiring to publish that any of the stocks specifically named are to-day tainted with this disease, for in every such instance the malady has been stamped out, and the herd can now be certified sound. I adduce them mainly as undeniable outbreaks occurring in the herds of men so well known that no one interested in the subject can have any difficulty in attesting their truth for himself. Let the objectors try to disprove these. There are plenty more such, not only in the past but to-day. The recent cases in Chester County, Pennsylvania, which have been sufficiently identified, a single diseased lung in particular cases having weighed 50 pounds in place of 3 pounds.

OUR EXISTING LUNG PLAGUE IMPORTED.

But some will even deny that the disease now prevalent on our Eastern seaboard is the genuine lung plague of Europe. Well, it was unknown in America until 1843, when Peter Dunn, of Brooklyn, bought an English cow from the ship Washington. This cow died in a few weeks of this lung affection, and the disease quickly spread to Dunn's other cows and to those of his neighbors, including the stables of the Skillman street distillery, where it continued until 1862, and was recognized by Dr. Thayer

NATIONAL CONVENTION OF CATTLE BREEDERS.

and the other members of the Massachusetts commission. William Meakim, of Bushwick, had his herd infected in 1849 by a yoke of oxen employed in drawing grain from the Brooklyn distilleries, and lost 40 head in three months, and from 6 to 10 head yearly for twenty years thereafter, when he gave up the business. This brings it down to 1869. Since that date I have been frequently consulted about the disease, not in New York only, but also in the adjoining States on the south, and occasionally in Connecticut.

WHY HAS THE PLAGUE NOT EXTENDED WEST.

From New York the plague has extended 200 miles in a southward direction, and to-day holds its ground and continues to extend as opportunity offers. It has followed this direction simply because the traffic in live stock has been active from New York to the large cities in the South, and because in and around those large cities it has found that constant interchange of animals and intermingling of herds which insures its perpetuation by presenting an endless succession of fresh and susceptible subjects. The same extension would have taken place over all the large manufacturing cities of New England, but for the careful guardianship of the cattle commission of Connecticut, who, through all the years since the disease was imported, have been called upon at frequent intervals to stamp out circumscribed fires of infection lit up by importations from New York. The plague has not extended westward mainly because there has been so little cattle traffic in that direction. It would have been financial folly at any early time to send common cattle west from the great Eastern cities, and, thanks to the Alleghanies, there is no large city within 200 miles of New York in that direction that would draw upon the market of the latter for dairy cows, or that was calculated to keep up the disease by the constant intermingling of herds.

The dangers from thorough-bred cattle sent West were incomparably greater, but various conditions served to reduce the risks of infection by this channel. First. Thorough-breds were usually better guarded against danger of contamination, not being sold in the common stock-yards. Second. Their owners are usually r. sponsible and honorable men, who would be little likely to sell at the current high market rates animals they knew to be infected. Third. Thorough-breds are always sold with pedigree, and the buyer is fully acquainted with the position and standing of the seller, so that in case of a sale of infected animals the breeder would have been constantly subject to an action for damages. Fourth. Until recently thorough-bred cattle were comparatively seldom sent west to our unfenced pasturages, so that if some did carry infection into new herds, the latter were still on well-fenced farms, and were kept rigidly apart from other stock to secure the purity of the breed, and thus the infection had a good chance to attack all the herd and to die out for lack of fresh susceptible subjects.

Such an immunity of a country in close proximity to an infected one is not at all unprecedented. Europe furnishes an exact parallel. For centuries the lung plague has prevailed in Central Europe, where it is kept up by the active cattle traffic and the constant importations from the infected East. But Spain and Portugal, on the south, and Scandinavia, on the north, being out of the line of direct traffic, keep clear to the present day—the few invasions of the northern nations having been easily repelled by prompt isolation and slaughter, while the less enterprising Southern Peninsula has not even once been called upon to suppress an outbreak.

OUR DANGERS INCREASING.

But our dangers of to-day are far greater than they have been in the past. Tens and hundreds of thoroughbred cattle are being constantly shipped to the West, and the great demand is for the unfenced ranges of the plains and beyond them. There the disease once introduced would find all those favorable conditions which have perpetuated it for centuries in the steppes of Eastern Europe and Asia, in spite of the best efforts of scientists, aided by the ungrudging support of the Government. These conditions are identical with those of Australia, where the disease has defied every effort to extirpate it, though they were carried out almost regardless of expense and of the numbers of animals that might have to be slaughtered. In New Zealand and South Africa the experience has been the same; the plague once planted on unfenced ranges, pastured in common by large herds, the property of different owners, has perpetuated itself in spite of every effort of man to suppress it.

Nor is our danger alone from thorough-bred cattle. The great investments in cattle from the plains and the consequent enhanced prices have established a trade in common stock for the supply of the Western ranches, and young stock are extensively shipped from the Middle and Eastern States to meet the demand. In years past the losses on the ventures in young calves have served to check the trade, but I regret to say it still continues to a considerable extent, and every such shipment is pregnant with danger.

If there were any hope of the extinction of the lung plague after it had reached our unfenced pasturages we might find some excuse for those who would have us close our eyes to the danger; but when it threatens us with the infliction of a tax of $50,000,000 to $200,000,000 a year, a tax which must increase in ratio with the increase of our herds, and which no statesmanship and no financial ability can ever hope to arrest or abolish, we cannot but consider him as an enemy of his country and of humanity who would counsel or encourage apathy or inaction. Who would cry "peace! peace!!" while a remorseless enemy is at our doors, and his emissaries and battalions are even in our midst, ready to seize our strongholds? Who would claim health when the cancer was eating into the tissues and slowly extending toward the vitals? Who would claim security when the deadly cobra had been roused and had coiled himself for his fatal spring?

If I speak strongly it is because I see the full measure of our danger; it is because I have traced the history of this disease in all historic time, and can speak from the unvarying experience of successive centuries and of different hemispheres; it is because I have been honored with a great trust in this matter, and because I would be recreant to that trust, to the country, to my profession, and to myself, if I failed to give warning where danger threatens, and reassurance where our course is safe.

MEASURES FOR SUPPRESSION AND EXTINCTION.

In devising means for suppressing any plague we must give paramount attention to two considerations: First. Can we render the animal system *insusceptible* or *nonreceptive of the poison?* and second, *can we destroy every vestige of the poison?* If we can perfectly accomplish either of these objects there will be an end of the plague at such a place. No plague can be propagated in the absence of susceptible subjects. No plague can survive if we destroy all its germs. The lung-plague virus is perfectly harmless to a community of horses, sheep, or swine. So it is to a great extent to cattle that have already passed through the disease and fully recovered. Just as a man does not readily contract small-pox a second time, so an ox does not usually suffer a second time from lung plague. I would not trouble you with this part of the subject but that some advocate the restriction of this plague by producing this comparative insusceptibility in the animals exposed.

METHODS OF SEEKING INSUSCEPTIBILITY.

This insusceptibility to lung plague may be attained more or less perfectly by various methods.

1st. *Keeping insusceptible breeds.*—Some breeds appear to be somewhat less receptive of lung plague than others. In some this has been acquired by a prolonged exposure of their ancestors to the plague, until the more susceptible strains of blood have died out, leaving only those that have a greater power of resistance to the contagion. This is merely "a survival of the fittest." In other cases cattle that are defective in muscular development, in loose connective tissue, and in the lymphatic apparatus, show a somewhat diminished susceptibility, as compared with those of an opposite habit of body. But in neither of these cases is the susceptibility ever completely eradicated from the race or family. Either of these conditions will to a slight extent reduce the losses, but neither separately nor together can they arrest the propagation of the poison nor prevent the progress of the disease. They are therefore only to be adopted as restrictive measures on open unfenced pasture ranges, covered with cattle, where the permanence of the disease is already assured and where no hope of its extinction can be held out. In other circumstances we can do incomparably better.

2d. *Passage of the young through the disease.*—In badly infected districts shrewd dairymen have profitably resorted to the expedient of exposing calves to the infection, realizing that the pecuniary loss through the death of the individual animal at this age was small, while the survivors could afterward be exposed to infection with impunity.

3d. *Inoculation with fresh virus from the diseased lung.*—A more economical method is the inoculation of the susceptible cattle in the tail so as to exhaust their susceptibility. This, when properly managed, does not cause a loss of over 1 or 2 per cent., and the survivors acquire as perfect an immunity from lung plague as vaccinated people do from small-pox. This inoculation is extensively practiced in Belgium and France, is obligatory in Holland, and is almost universal in Australia, Tasmania, New Zealand, South Africa, and certain parts of Great Britain and America. It has greatly diminished the losses in these countries but in no one of them has it put an end to the plague. In the city of Edinburgh, where it is supplemented by the slaughter of the sick, and where it was loudly claimed that it had extinguished the disease. I found on my recent visit that the abattoir was furnishing frequent examples of lungs from city dairy cows with the characteristic lesions of lung plague. In Holland, where the compulsory inoculation is also supplemented by slaughter of the sick, the fat cattle from the great feeding stables frequently furnish, when killed, the unmistakable lung lesions of this disease, nor is this at all surprising. The inoculated poison propagated in the tissues of the tail not only protects the individual system but also secures the multiplication of the germs and their preservation in the stables, so that when an animal freshly introduced and inoculated fails to take, and to be protected, it has every opportunity of contracting the disease in the ordinary way, in the lungs. The same result obtains where inoculation is practiced on a large scale on cattle in open pasturages. Mr. Watson states as the result of his experience in Australia and New Zealand that on the occasions on which large herds of thousands or tens of thousands had been inoculated, a certain number of animals always failed to be brought in, and among these uninoculated animals there was in every case a very heavy percentage of loss after they had mingled with the inoculated. Mr. Corbet gives the same testimony concerning his experience in Natal. "The disease," he says, "is always lurking about and introduced to a greater or less extent each time of inoculation."

This is the great objection to inoculation as usually practiced. It is a means of multiplying the disease germs, and while it protects the inoculated animal it furnishes material for the infection of every susceptible animal that may be brought in contact with it or with the premises where it has been. Inoculation is admissible as a means of self-protection by the individual owner in cases where the Government or local authorities take no efficient steps for the stamping out of the disease; but it is bad policy when our object is the complete extinction of the malady and when we are adopting other measures well calculated to secure this end. One suggestion more on this subject is, that from herds in which inoculation is permitted no animal should be allowed to pass out except to immediate slaughter. The premises become infected and the inmates may carry the infection on the surface of their bodies as well as in the lungs.

4th. *Inoculation with weakened virus.*—The application of the method of Pasteur of inoculation with attenuated virus is advocated by some, but it is liable to all the objections urged against the simple inoculation. .The attenuated virus is weakened, not sterilized; the germs continue to propagate their kind, and as their virulence has been lessened by culture under certain conditions, it can be enhanced by culture under conditions of an opposite kind. All such measures, which owe their efficacy to the propagation in the animal system of the diseased germ we seek to destroy, are to be deprecated and discarded whenever more radical measures of extinction can be adopted.

5th. *Inoculation with sterilized virus.*—Two years ago I was led by my study of the manifestations of the lung plague in the system to suspect that the immunity, after a first attack, was acquired not by the contact of the living germ with the lung tissue, but of its chemical products or excretions. I accordingly took measures to kill the germ without altering the chemical condition of the virulent fluid, and inoculated the sterilized liquid on the susceptible animal. In ten animals into which this liquid was injected there occurred no local swelling such as results from the inoculation with the living germ, and no one of these animals had local swellings, when afterward, inoculated with fresh virus containing living germs, nor had any lung plague when exposed for six months in infected herds and premises. In every case in which I tested the animals thus protected, by inoculating them with fresh living germs, I took the precaution of inoculating at the same time an unprotected subject, and in every such animal the disease appeared in a characteristic form; and when the inoculation had been made on the soft, loose tissues of the flank, in a fatal one. I have since learned by experiments on animals that had already stood some time in infected buildings, that this inoculation with sterilized lymph is not protective of animals that have already taken the germs into their lungs. To be effective it must be practiced on cattle before they have been exposed to the contagion; and its efficiency will be enhanced by a repetition after an interval of a week or more.

This method, it will be observed, obviates the main objections to inoculation. By it there is no germ introduced into the animal system, nor any laid up in the buildings where inoculated beasts are kept. The method therefore may be safely applied to one of a score or a hundred susceptible cattle without endangering the rest, and the building where a thousand cattle have been operated on in this way may be at once filled with as many more fresh and susceptible animals without disinfection, and yet without any danger of evil consequences.

The method is therefore immeasurably superior to any other that has been hitherto proposed, and in special cases may be resorted to with excellent results.

The objections to its exclusive use are those that apply to all measures that come short of a speedy extinction of the disease: 1st. The keeping of diseased animals for the production of the virus is not without its dangers. 2d. The application of the method over a wide district is necessarily slow. 3d. The application to infected districts, extending over six different States, would entail a vast amount of machinery, and the perfection of the work would suffer in various ways; operators would fail for lack of care or ability; cattle would escape notice and afterwards fall victims to the disease: and the incessant additions of susceptible animals by birth and otherwise would present a serious difficulty. 4th. To operate on animals most satisfactorily it must be done before they enter the infected herds, and this would necessitate places of detention for such store animals outside the infected districts, and a considerable additional delay and outlay in cattle traffic. 5th. The expense for all this machinery would be largely prohibitory of the practice. 6th. Finally, we cannot expect of this any more than of any other inoculation, that it will prove absolutely protective in every case. We meet with second attacks of small-pox, measles, and even of lung plague. We cannot therefore hope that we shall be able to absolutely protect such exceptional animals as have a great inherent susceptibility to the lung plague. These exceptional cases forbid that we should adopt this as an exclusive method when we can resort to one that is absolutely certain in its results. This method may be of the greatest value for the protection of individual herds where there is no governmental measure for stamping out, and it may be conjoined with the ordinary method of extinction by slaughter without that danger of propagating the disease which always attaches to ordinary inoculation; but with all the many advantages which I can see in this, my own system, I am convinced that the Government can do incomparably better if it will.

6th. *Preventive medication.*—In my experience of this disease in Great Britain, over twenty years ago, I found that a long course of certain tonics, and notably of the preparations of iron, fortified the system so that few animals fell victims to the contagion. But in this as in the other methods named the result is imperfect, and the protected animals soon reacquire the susceptibility after the tonic has been withdrawn.

DESTRUCTION OF THE POISON.

1st. *By disinfection of the air breathed.*—In many instances of infected herds I have found that a thorough fumigation with sulphur fumes for half an hour at a time, twice or better three times a day, has at once put a stop to the further extension of the infection. The cattle already infected would still suffer, but for the others the poison was destroyed before or soon after it entered the air-passages, and before it could make its way into the tissues, and no disease resulted. Like the other methods named this has its drawbacks. It requires suitable buildings and careful manipulation to secure a sufficient effect without danger to the animals, and as it requires such frequent application, it must be left in the hands of attendants who cannot always be relied on to carry it out safely and effectively.

2d. *By isolation, slaughter, and disinfection.*—Wherever the movement and intermingling of cattle can be prevented or sufficiently controlled, the method of stamping out by isolation, slaughter, and disinfection has ever been attended by the most perfect success. It has been ineffective in countries like Australia, where endless herds of cattle roam over the fenceless plains, but wherever lands are inclosed and where movement can be arrested or controlled, as in Norway, Sweden, Denmark, Oldenburg, Switzerland, and Massachusetts, it has resulted in the complete eradication of the malady. In New York in 1879 the same measures rooted out the disease from four of the eight infected counties, and restricted it to eight herds, which were temporarily preserved for lack of funds in two more counties, while in Kings County and the adjacent part of Queens, where local authorities had successfully opposed our work, the malady remained widely prevalent. While advocating the full efficacy of this method, it is needless to go into minor particulars further than to say that no additions from the public markets should be allowed to herds in infected districts, and that all additions to such herds, apart from natural increase, should be by special license from healthy districts, or from close markets which receive cattle only from such healthy districts; that every death in a herd in such proclaimed infected district should be promptly reported, and the carcass examined by a veterinary inspector; that no cattle should be moved from such herds in infected districts except to immediate slaughter, where examination of the carcass can be made by a veterinary inspector; or such movement should only be allowed after the herd and district have been certified by the inspector to have been sound and without dangerous additions for six months; that all infected animals, or far better, every infected herd, should be promptly slaughtered, and that a thorough disinfection should be made of all premises where infected animals have been.

I have always held that the only sound and just method of dealing with this disease must be directed and sustained by the National Government. I quote from my monograph on the lung plague, published in 1879:

"The plague threatens to reach our southern and western ranges, whence it will be as impossible to eradicate it as from the Russian steppes, Australia, and South Africa, and from which continuous accessions of infection will be thrown upon our Middle and Eastern States, and shall we hesitate to call upon the National Government to interfere? This is a question of incomparably more moment to the Western and Middle States than to Delaware, Maryland, or Virginia. To throw the burden of the extinction of this disease on these States is as impolitic as it is unjust. If ever there was a question which, in its future bearing, affected the United States, as a whole, it is this.

"It would be highly appropriate that the agriculturists of the different States, Western and Southern as well as Eastern, should petition Congress to take this matter up and adopt such measures as would forever rid our country of this most insidious of all animal plagues. At all hazards the work ought to be done, and that speedily. If State rights stand in the way, let the money at least be supplied, as it rightfully ought. from the national exchequer, and applied by the different States through their own officials under the supervision of some responsible Department— say the Agricultural Department, a live stock disease commission, the National Board of Health, or even the Treasury Department. It is folly and worse to quarrel about the means until the plague shall have passed beyond control. Action is wanted, of a prompt and decisive nature, by the General Government or with its assistance, and those who are most deeply interested in the subject should press this upon the Government until such action shall have been secured."

I would only add that, in my opinion, the Federal Government should provide and pay its own inspectors to act as experts in all the infected States, while the sheriffs or other State officials should conduct them into the herds to be examined, and, on behalf of the State. see to the appraisement and slaughter of all herds pronounced to be infected, to the safe disposal of the carcasses, and to the thorough disinfection of the premises. The sheriffs or other State officials should further deliver the certificates of such appraisements to the federal inspector, who should forward the same to the federal authority at Washington, and he should communicate with the owner of the herd, and on receipt of a signed receipt for the amount, should pay him the amount of indemity for the animals slaughtered.

Mr. CHORN, of Kentucky. With the permission of Mr. Smith, the chairman of the committee on order of business, I wish to offer a resolution that we adjourn until 5 o'clock this evening, if that is in order, so that we can have those people here with us who are all vitally interested in these discussions.

The PRESIDENT *pro tempore* (Professor MORROW). I would suggest that you put your motion in the form of a reconsideration of the vote which has already fixed the time for meeting.

Mr. CHORN. Then I move that we reconsider that vote.

The motion to reconsider was agreed to.

Mr. CHORN. Now, I renew my motion to adjourn until 5 o'clock.

Mr. CAREY, of Wyoming. There appears to be conflicting interests here. I am aware that many of the men who have come here are in attendance upon these stock sales, but we do hope that we shall devote all the time that we can until we attain the object of this meeting. Now, of course, there are a number of scientific articles that are to be read before this Convention, and we are anxious to hear them; but the final outcome of this meeting is what we are really anxious about. That means the appointment of a committee to go to Washington and lobby through Congress such measures as we deem necessary in our interest. I think that Senator Williams struck the key-note when he said that there must be a committee appointed who are willing to work, who are willing to pay their expenses, who are willing to give this matter sufficient time to have measures adopted that will accomplish something. Now we want a meeting this afternoon. If 3.30 is too early, why not say 4 o'clock ? We can have a meeting before this evening, and these gentlemen can read their articles. Now, as I understand, there is a meeting this evening that will interfere ; to-morrow there is a sale, and if we have to adjourn this meeting and let the stock sales take place, instead of going on, we will not be able to finish our work for a week. I therefore move an amendment that when we adjourn we adjourn until 4 o'clock.

Mr. CHORN, of Kentucky. There are many of the very best breeders in this meeting who are directly and vitally interested in these stock sales. They cannot get here at 4 o'clock, but they can get here at 5 o'clock. We will be here at that hour and will give this important meeting our heartiest support, and we do beg for 5 o'clock.

Mr. CAREY, of Wyoming. Say 4.30, then. [Laughter.]

The amendment was not agreed to, and the motion of Mr. Chorn was carried.

The PRESIDENT *pro tempore.* I beg to suggest the importance of the appointment of a committee on resolutions. I happen to know that there are likely to be a few resolutions which will conflict, some of them at least, with our purposes and views, and such a committee could consider these and report to this body.

Professor ROBERTS, of New York. I move that the chair appoint a committee of three on resolutions.

A DELEGATE. I move to amend by inserting five.

The amendment was accepted, and the motion as amended was agreed to.

The PRESIDENT *pre tempore.* The chair will name Professor Roberts as the chairman of that committee, and will reserve the appointment of the others until we meet again.

Professor ROBERTS. The chair will please excuse me. I have more business than I can well attend to now. It will be inconvenient for me to serve. For one member of that committee I will suggest Professor Law.

The PRESIDENT *pro tempore.* The chair will reserve, if you please, the appointment of the committee until later.

A DELEGATE. I move we now adjourn.

The motion was agreed to, and at 1 o'clock and 3 minutes the Convention adjourned.

The Convention met pursuant to adjournment, Senator Williams, the president, in the chair.

The PRESIDENT. Just before adjournment provision was made for the appointment of a committee on resolutions, with the intention of having referred to it all resolutions that may be offered by gentlemen, and to be by that committee reported to the Convention with its recommendations. That committee will consist of Messrs. Sanders, of Illinois; Chorn, of Kentucky; W. T. Smith, of Iowa; Bonham, of Ohio; and Redfield, of New York. I will announce now that Dr. Salmon, of the Department of Agriculture, has been commissioned by Dr. Loring to read a paper at this Convention, and if there is nothing further requiring the immediate action of the meeting I would suggest that we now listen to Dr. Salmon.

Dr. SALMON then presented the following paper:

PREVENTION OF CONTAGIOUS DISEASES OF ANIMALS IN AMERICA.

Among the many questions connected with the contagious diseases of animals those most suitable for discussion at this Convention are the ones which are nearest related to the subject of prevention. There are still too many people who cling to old ideas of the origin and nature of contagious diseases. Our popular writers still teach that they are the result of the "absorption of foul matter from impure air, and that good ventilation and pure air are specific preventives." Good ventilation and pure air are excellent things, but if they are specific preventives how can we explain the cases of glanders which occur among horses that seldom see the inside of a stable; the cases of hog cholera in the open fields, and of chicken cholera among fowls which are never housed?

Other writers—and their name is legion—tell us that the origin of hog cholera, for instance, is easily explained by the conditions under which hogs are raised, particularly in the West. Large numbers are kept together; they have the reprehensible habit of crowding each other to an uncomfortable degree in their sleeping places; they have so little regard for hygienic rules as to lie two or three deep. As a necessary consequence the under hog breathes terribly impure air; he even inspires so much dust that this alone would cause inflammation of the lungs. Couple this with his injudicious and irregular diet, and the origin of hog cholera is so clear that our friends are abundantly satisfied; they rather object to additional evidence for fear of unsettling beliefs now held with the most implicit confidence. We are even told that foot-and-mouth disease is as indigenous to England as the fogs and mists; that it always exists and always will, because it is provoked by the climate and the manner of keeping the cattle.

But these remarkable conclusions are not so much the result of a long period of observations on the diseases themselves—they are rather the outcome of meditations as to what ought to be. "Our enormous and well-appointed army," said the French about 1870, "will have no trouble in marching victoriously into Berlin;" but since the investigation of the size and equipment of that army was made in the office and not in the field, it resulted in a slight change of programme, which brought the German army to Paris and made the Frenchmen prisoners of war. And if we accept too hastily the conclusions to which I have referred—conclusions based upon an insufficient knowledge of these diseases, we also may invite disaster. The inflammation of the lungs seen in hog cholera is not a simple inflammation, due to mechanical irritation by inert particles of dust; the ulcers of the intestines are not the simple results of indigestion; the discharge and ulceration of glanders cannot be produced by lack of ventilation alone, nor the fever and eruption of foot-and-mouth disease by damp, and cold, and mud. These are contagious diseases, and an animal exposed to the virus contracts the disease, no matter what its conditions of life, just as your child contracts measles or scarlet fever when exposed to them, though it dwells in a palace, with the most perfect diet and surroundings. Hog cholera has been introduced into the South within the last thirty years, and now it is an annual scourge; but there is the same old breed of hogs, and they are allowed to roam at their own sweet will, just as has been the custom from time immemorial. If sleeping too many in a bed produces hog cholera to-day why did it not have the same effect thirty or forty years ago?

And so with chicken cholera. By making an insignificant wound with a lancet dipped in virus, or even by giving the virus with the food, I can destroy the greater part of the fowls upon any farm, and I care not what are the conditions of life or the quality of the food.

Is pleuro-pneumonia produced by cold, bad feed, or filthy and unventilated stables? If so, why is it not found around some of your Western cities—Cincinnati, Saint Louis, Chicago? Surely the cow that kicked the lamp, that spilled the oil, that fired the straw, that burned the stable, &c., was not the last instance of improper stabling in or about this great city. And yet in many parts of Europe they talk about pleuro-pneumonia originating from improper conditions of life pretty much as our learned friends tell us that glanders, and hog cholera and chicken cholera and the rest of the list, originate in this country.

Then there is rinderpest and sheep-pox and foot-and-mouth disease abroad, decimating the flocks and herds year after year and causing incalculable losses. Why do not these diseases appear as regularly among the animals upon our own grazing lands? Is it because there is something unfavorable to these diseases in our climate, or is it because the contagia—the germs—of those plagues have never yet been disseminated over our territory? There is not a particle of doubt in my mind that rinderpest, sheep pox, and epizootic aptha would sweep America as they have swept Europe were they once fairly introduced among our animals.

The truth seems to be, with most if not all of the contagious fevers, that every case is produced directly or indirectly from germs which were developed by a case which preceded it, just as every crop of corn is produced by seed from a preceding crop. I care not how well you prepare your ground, how favorable you make the conditions of life, you cannot get a crop of corn without seed; so a contagious fever is the result of the development of a living organism in the animal body, and you can no more get a crop of that organism without seed than you can the crop of corn.

Just here I am usually met with an argument, apparently looked upon as invulnerable, forever demonstrating the spontaneous production of animal plagues. These diseases, it is said, could not always have been contracted from pre-existing cases for the very reason that some time in the remote past there were no pre-existing animals—there must have been a first case of disease. No doubt of it; but this is one of those philosophical considerations which is not as practical as it appears upon its face. So, too, there must have been a first grain of corn, a first pig, a first sheep, a first calf; but let the young farmer of to-day put his land in the most favorable condition possible and set upon the fence expecting the origin de novo of his corn, his pigs, his sheep, and his cattle—you know that he might sit there until his hair was white and his eyes dim with age without seeing such a phenomenon; no, not if his farm took in a continent and his field of vision embraced it all. And if the contagious organisms were as large as cattle, sheep, or pigs, or even as grains of corn, so that their goings and comings might be traced as we can trace these things, there would be no more question of the origin of glanders and hog cholera from the conditions of life than there is of cattle from the grass of your fields or corn from your fertile soil. Contagious fevers, then, are caused by specific germs, and so long as animals are exposed to these a considerable proportion will sicken and die in spite of hygienic surroundings, in spite of good and proper food, unless they are granted an immunity by methods analogous to vaccination.

During the last decade we have had some of the most brilliant investigations and some of the most important discoveries that are to be found in the whole history of medicine; that greatest of all mysteries which enveloped contagious diseases in impenetrable darkness during the long ages of the past has at last, so far as concerns a number of these, been entirely solved. The cause of these diseases has been traced to microscopic organisms; to living things, capable of wonderfully rapid growth and multiplication, which can be seen and cultivated and studied. And by such studies we have learned that these organisms—germs if you please—may be made to change their nature and produce a mild, instead of a fatal attack, from which the animal recovers and is enabled in the future to resist this virus even in its most malignant form. We have here a method, mysterious as the disease, which the omniscient Creator has provided that may be successful when all others have failed or where no others are applicable. It gives us hope that in the near future we shall have efficient means for practically controlling the greater part of these destructive plagues.

But to-day, gentlemen, as we review these diseases one by one, and consider the means which we have at hand for their suppression, we cannot doubt that they are yet, as they have been in the past, the most important and the most difficult problems which have engaged the attention of mankind, and that they will tax our intelligence and our ingenuity to the utmost before all the difficulties connected with them are overcome. With a single disease the new method of vaccination introduced by the illustrious Pasteur has proved successful in practice, and this success has been due to a character of stability in the virus which exists with but one other non-recurrent disease so far as our investigations have gone. Before this method can be applied to other diseases, and particularly to those with which we are most interested, there are new problems to be solved not less intricate and just as hard to grasp as were those so lately conquered. The direction has been pointed out to us, but the way is not open.

CHICKEN CHOLERA

is one of the most widely distributed diseases, and certainly causes enormous aggregate losses. It is now as well understood as any of our contagious diseases, and it is one of the few in which the germs have been discovered and carefully studied. These germs under ordinary conditions must be taken into the stomach with the food or drink to produce their effects, and consequently by a proper use of disinfectants the disease may be almost entirely prevented. Fowls may also be made insusceptible to cholera by vaccination with a feeble virus, or by inoculation with a diluted virus. A few investigations to determine the best method of putting up the virus, and there is no doubt but that it could be sent to every part of the country in such a form that any one could use it.

BLACK-QUARTER

is another disease which is very destructive in localities of nearly every State in the Union. This has been recently investigated with much success in France, and we are told that it may be certainly prevented by both inoculation and vaccination.

HOG CHOLERA.

With hog cholera our investigations, owing to the difficulty of the subject, have not reached such satisfactory results. The germ has been isolated, cultivated, and studied, but not sufficiently to make us master of the conditions upon which the virulence depends. As I have cultivated it, it is one of the most unstable of viruses. The germ is easily cultivated, but its effects are far from uniform: a second, or third, or even fourth cultivation may produce fatal results, but it gradually loses its virulence until large quantities have no effect. During this diminution of virulence we get a vaccine which produces a mild attack and grants immunity, but it has been impossible to make this vaccine multiply itself without becoming too weak to be effectual, and it has been equally impossible to preserve it at the required strength a sufficient length of time to make its use practical over a very large section of the country. I do not say that this obstacle will not be overcome in the future; on the other hand, I am sanguine that it will be. We are just completing our arrangements at Washington to give this and our other contagious diseases a thorough investigation, and I can only say that, in spite of the assertion of Pasteur, until we learn more in regard to the virus vaccination cannot be used safely, nor is it sure to confer the desired immunity.

Separation and disinfection are then the measures which must be depended upon for the present. These are already largely practiced in many parts of the country, and have been the means of saving millions of dollars' worth of hogs since the first investigations of the Department of Agriculture demonstrated beyond question the contagiousness of the disease. There are still undoubtedly heavy losses which cannot be prevented in this way, and for such losses there appears to be but one practical remedy, and that is vaccination. Either we must fold our hands and allow the loss to go on as at present unchecked, or we must study the germs and master this secret of nature which will make vaccination a possibility.

SOUTHERN OR TEXAS CATTLE FEVER.

When we commenced the investigation of this disease a few years ago there was but ittle known of the district from which cattle would disseminate the infection; there was a vague and somewhat uncertain idea, that the whole Gulf coast might be a dangerous district, but it was universally acknowledged that wherever there was frost and snow there the contagion of Texas fever could not survive, and cattle coming from such districts could be safely introduced upon our northern ranges. To-day we know that the infected district extends hundreds of miles from the Gulf coast, that in the East we may reach it by crossing the Rappahannock River in Virginia, that it is. a long way this side of the line of frost and snow, and that, worse than all, it is advancing, slowly it is true, but steadily, surely advancing towards the best and most heavily stocked grazing lands in the country.

In making this statement it is my desire to avoid the character of the mere alarmist. There is no occasion for immediate apprehension except in a few States, but there is occasion for immediate action. The advance of this disease can only be checked by laws regulating the movements of cattle, and with our present knowledge it is absurd to think of doing it in any other way. If the States along the border line of the infected district would adopt a law doing away with fences and consequently compel the owners of stock to prevent its running at large, and at the same time prohibit the driving of cattle from the infected to the uninfected district the advance of the disease would probably be arrested. As it is, an enormous territory has become infected, which comprises a considerable part of Virginia, two-thirds of North Carolina, the whole of South Carolina, Georgia, Florida, Alabama, Mississippi, Louisiana, the greater part of Texas and Arkansas, and a large section in Tennessee. It will be instructive for every one interested in the American cattle industry to take a map of the United States and compare the part infected with this disease with that which is still free from it. Such a proceeding is well calculated to inspire an appreciation of the importance of giving this subject early and careful attention.

GLANDERS.

This disease, which causes at times such heavy losses with horses, and which produces a most horrible, loathsome, and fatal disorder in people, is now very inadequately dealt with in this country. Some States have no laws whatever in regard to it, and in most of the others they are imperfect, ineffectual, or not enforced. I have in mind now a case in a State where there is even a commission for suppressing this class of diseases. Some here will no doubt recognize it in the brief allusion which follows. Two horses were pronounced glandered by one or more veterinarians and quarantined by the State commission. As another practitioner considered the cases doubtful the highest talent in the American profession was consulted and inoculation experiments were made. A half dozen veterinarians unhesitatingly pronounced the disease to be glanders; the inoculation experiments proved this beyond question. In spite of this, however, the horses, instead of being slaughtered, were placed on pasture, the lesions of the disease were hidden by long and continued treatment, and then the owner goes to the legislature and obtains damages from the State for false quarantine. As a fitting climax to this absurd legal miscarriage these same horses were recently exhibited at the State fair, whether to show how easy it is to evade the laws in that State or whether to advertise the smartness of the owners it is difficult to say.

Certainly with such a disease as this we should have effectual laws in every State, and when an animal is pronounced glandered by the State veterinarian it should be destroyed at once. No matter if the symptoms are mild—no matter if there is a remote chance of covering them up or even of curing the animal; that animal is a center of infection from which new cases will arise. It is a source of danger to human beings; it is a nuisance which ought not to be tolerated under any circumstances.

PLEURO-PNEUMONIA.

It is but a few months ago that the United States Department of Agriculture was charged with estimating the direct annual losses in this country from pleuro-pneumonia alone at $66,000,000. We were also charged with having published the statement that this disease had crossed the Missouri River and was affecting the great herds which roam the Western plains. That story unfortunately crossed the ocean. It went to the foreign markets of American beef; it was copied in the journals there as coming from the American Department of Agriculture, and you can judge for yourselves whether or not it had a tendency to remove any of the restrictions and obstacles which have been placed in the way of our exporters. Although the assertion was promptly contradicted abroad, it has not, so far as I am aware, received any public notice at home, and I only refer to the matter here for the purpose of stating that no one could have been more surprised at its publication than we were at the Department, for neither this statement nor anything resembling it has ever found its way into any of the Department publications.

The time has come for speaking plainly in regard to the extent and losses from pleuro-pneumonia. I have never believed nor do I believe to day that anything is gained in the long run by attempting to cover up the existence of a contagious disease by whitewashing reports or by any other form of deception. And, on the other hand, I must admit that I see no virtue in exaggeration, nothing but harm in the reports of enormous losses from pleuro-pneumonia and of its existence hither and yon in thirty different States which it has never entered. So far from the direct losses from this disease reaching up into the millions, it would undoubtedly be an exaggeration to say that they amount to one hundred thousand dollars a year. So far from its having reached the Western plains, there has never been a case found west of the Alleghany Mountains having the remotest resemblance to this plague, notwithstanding a pretty thorough ransacking of that great territory. And east of the Alleghanies, if you except a single farm in Connecticut, a half dozen farms in Pennsylvania, and perhaps a dozen in New Jersey, it may be truthfully said that there are no evidences of this disease at present beyond the immediate vicinity of a few large cities : New York, Brooklyn, Newark, Baltimore, and possibly Washington.

Just what the situation is in these cities nothing but a thorough inspection will ever reveal. Brooklyn and Baltimore have a very bad reputation, but there have certainly been exaggerations in regard to the condition of the former. Taking the matter at the worst, I think it is evident that it would not be a herculean task to free ourselves from all suspicion of this foreign intruder. With energy and perseverance, a force of men who are able to identify this disease when they see it, and a very reasonable expenditure of money, we may be assured that the plague could be exterminated. But what are to be the details of this undertaking? Where is the money to come from? How is it to be used? Who should direct the work? How are they to get the necessary powers? These are questions which might be profitably discussed in this Convention, and if a practical scheme can be perfected, I doubt not it will be productive of much good.

If I have left many points untouched and treated others in a superficial manner it is because I am unwilling to take more of your time than is absolutely necessary. I am anxious above all things that those most directly interested, those who put their money and their time in the live stock industry shall speak on these questions. I have no individual opinions or theories to inflict upon you, but the position with which I have been honored has given me means of securing information which few others possess, and it is my earnest desire to give such evidence as may be needed to prevent the acceptance on the one hand of the extreme views of those who tell us that there are no dangerous diseases in the country, and on the other hand of those who insist that pleuro-pneumonia is ravaging an enormous territory, that other diseases are increasing from month to month by a sort of geometrical progression, and that our whole country is one great hotbed of disease.

I wish also to assure you that the United States Department of Agriculture fully appreciates the importance and is greatly interested in this subject of contagious animal diseases, and that it is willing, anxious, determined to do everything in its power to assist the stock owners of America in protecting their animals from these dreadful plagues.

The PRESIDENT *pro tempore* (Professor MORROW). I would ask if the committee on order of business has any further report to make, to add to that submitted at the morning session.

Mr. C. R. SMITH, of Iowa. We recommended this morning, in addition to the paper just read, that it be followed by a paper by Mr. Sanders, and we now recommend to follow the latter paper ten-minute practical speeches on this subject of pleuro-pneumonia by L. S. Coffin, Prof. J. D. Hopkins, Veterinarian, of Wyoming, J. M. Carey, and Mr. Crane, of New Jersey, to be followed by five-minute volunteer speeches on the subject. We have nothing further to recommend except that a thorough discussion and settlement of the subject of pleuro-pneumonia be had, and that no other subject be taken up until we have disposed of this one.

A DELEGATE. I move that we proceed in accordance with the recommendations of the committee.

The motion was agreed to.

Mr. SANDERS, of Illinois. Mr. Chairman, I do not know upon what authority or grounds any one felt authorized to say that I had prepared a paper to be read at this Convention. I have never told any one that I was going to read a paper here; no one ever asked me to do so, and I certainly have not prepared such a paper; and furthermore, I am in no kind of condition to make an extemporaneous talk to-night. I shall not attempt to inflict you with an address or lecture. There are one or two points that I merely wish to hint upon, which may serve as pointers to some extent for the discussions which may follow, and as my connection with the Treasury Cattle Commission has caused me to pay a great deal of attention especially to pleuro-pneumonia and the quarantine regulations during the past two years, I shall be happy to answer any questions on the subject. I wish to say that I am exceedingly pleased with the manner in which Dr. Salmon has presented the question of pleuro-pneumonia. It is precisely in accordance with my own observation and my own views. There is no doubt that there has been a wonderful amount of idle talk upon the subject. There have been alarmists all over the country, and as secretary of the Treasury Cattle Commision, the member to whom the communications come (excepting those sent to Professor Law by his own personal acquaintances), I am in constant receipt of letters. In this general correspondence you would be surprised to see the number of letters complaining of this disease, There has scarcely been a week—scarcely two days—since the Commission was appointed, that letters have not been received at my office from Wyoming, Texas, Illinois, and so on, stating that pleuro-pneumonia had broken out somewhere. We have had these alarms sent in from every quarter. Of course, I have felt it my duty to institute certain inquiries in relation to these reports, and in every case it has proven to be a false alarm. The disease was not pleuro-pneumonia. This accounts largely for the false alarm on the subject. The Treasury Cattle Commission has been engaged in ascertaining for the Treasury Department where the disease actually exists in this country. We found no evidence that it existed, or ever had, west of the Alleghany Mountains, and we so reported, and we found no evidence of the disease aside from the points mentioned by Professor Law in his address to-day and by Dr. Salmon. We have found that true, genuine, contagious disease does exist in this country along the Atlantic sea-board in a few localities, as was presented so ably by Professor Law to-day. The reason for the fortunate circumstance that there is none of this disease in the West, is because the tide has been toward the centers around which the disease exists, and not away from them. Around New York the great tide is toward the butcher shops, and these dairy-men about the great cities, who have been in the business a long time, know pleuro-pneumonia very well indeed, and just as soon as they find pleuro-pneumonia, their cattle go immediately to the butcher shops. This has very largely prevented the spread of the disease throughout the country. We found it existing in a number of these places. There is no question about its existence in New York, Brooklyn, New Jersey, some places at present in Pennsylvania, about Baltimore, and possibly about Washington. It has not spread to any alarming extent. The most forcible case is one that occurred in Pennsylvania this summer, and I wish Dr. Salmon had referred more to it. I allude to this simply to show that we have a precise knowledge as to where it exists, and also that there is a reason why the cattle men of the West, who are certainly free from this disease now, should feel some degree of this alarm. A gentleman bought some cattle in Baltimore in July last. A few of them were brought to Baltimore from Virginia, and put in the stock-yard at Baltimore, and a few others were brought from in and about the yards in Baltimore and were taken to Pennsylvania. They were sold in Chester, Delaware, and some other counties, and everywhere those animals went in about forty days pleuro-pneumonia appeared, and Dr. Salmon has told me he never saw the disease manifest a more distinct type; never saw a case where he was more satisfied, with the diagnosis. Supposing someone in the West had bought those cattle in Baltimore and brought them here, to our Chicago stock-yards, to be sent to Wyoming, Colorado, Kansas, and other States, what would have been the result! In Pennsylvania they are practically protected, as the State authority quarantines, and I presume there is not a particle of danger of its spreading.

Now, if I have not stated the case fairly, it is because my recollection is at fault, and Dr. Gadsden, who knows more about it, will correct me. I hear gentlemen make their astounding statements, and congratulate themselves that the West is entirely free from contagious disease, that the whole country is entirely free in fact, and that they are able to take cattle from one part to another part of the country. It may be well enough perhaps to say that the British authorities are just as well informed of the precise condition of cattle disease in this country as any of our own people. Their consuls in every State are specially charged with keeping close watch upon this subject; and every dispatch that goes into the Associated Press and every rumor that gets afloat is reported, and the facts, when they are ascertained to be facts, are also reported. The rumors are reported as well as the facts. Now, to say that we are free from disease in the West, for the simple purpose of affecting the British markets is perfectly useless. They know just as much about our Texas fever as we do. I was much surprised to hear the talk about the absolute freedom from contagious disease in Iowa. I have seen hundreds and hundreds of animals lying dead in that State which have died from Texas fever, and any one who has lived in Iowa as long as I have will bear me out in that statement of affairs there at one time. We cannot misrepresent the matter to them in any way, gentlemen, and if you attempt to do so when you do tell them the exact facts, they will get no credit over there. In England, last summer, in a long conversation with Professor Brown, who is the chief veterinary adviser of the privy council, and upon whose advice they act, said to me: "We are entirely satisfied that your whole country west of the Alleghanies is perfectly free from pleuro-pneumonia. We have no doubt of the ability of your cattle commission to arrange some plan by which cattle can be brought from the West, through northern lines of travel, and exported to Great Britain without any special danger of pleuro-pneumonia, but our legislation is such that we must regard your whole country as a nation. We don't know here anything about your States, or lines, or regulation; we only know from our own reports and from yours that what we call and know as pleuro-pneumonia exists with you as a nation, and under the act of Parliament the privy council is absolutely powerless to remove these restrictions in favor of the West, although we are sure it can be done with safety." I mention this to emphasize the point made by one speaker here to-day that this was a national affair, and that the proper power to take up and handle it was that of the General Government. We have been taking very strong measures during the past year to perfect a system of quarantine in order to prevent the further importation of animal plagues, and the condition of things in Great Britain has amply justified all the precaution we have taken. We have imported five times as many cattle as in any previous year in the history of the country, and there has never been a time when there has been so much foot and mouth disease as now. It is a most infectious disease. I am not a veterinary surgeon, but I know enough about it to know that it is a most dangerous thing, one to be dreaded; not because it is necessarily fatal and results in the decimation of the herd, but because it results in the loss of at least one year to the owner.

One more word. I know, Mr. Chairman, that there are many who have claimed that this was only a scare gotten up by veterinary surgeons in order to establish a business, and there are many who have that idea to-day. If they will go out one-half as much as I have and make examinations for themselves they will get over that notion sure. I said to Mr. Brown this year, "Is it not possible that you are mistaken as to the number of cases we have in the United States?" Said he, "I don't know, but I do know that we received five cases in the first six months of last year." "Then," said I, "Is it not possible you are mistaken in your diagnosis? Is it not acute pneumonia, or disease engendered by bad ventilation on shipboard?" Said he, "We have had too long and too costly an experience in Great Britain not to know pleuropneumonia when we see it. It is what we call contagious pleuropneumonia, and what we are going to continue to call contagious pleuropneumonia." Now we can make up our minds that Parliament will not change any law that it has enacted in favor of any section of this country. There is no question that we have this disease in isolated places along the coast, and we must with the aid of the General Government, by some process or other, take some steps to wipe it out. But *how* to do it is the difficulty. I remember when I first became connected with this matter, that I thought I could draw up a bill that would do the job. I tried my hand several times, but there are difficulties in the way—so many questions of State rights, and sovereignty and jurisdiction, and so many interests to consult that the man who is lawyer enough, and practical cattle man enough, and practical railroad man enough, and practical butcher enough, and practical veterinarian enough to draft a bill that will provide the elaborate machinery that, without clashing with State laws, will stamp out this disease is a bigger man, and a better lawyer, and a better cattle man and a better newspaper man than I am. [Laughter.]

Mr. LAWRENCE, of Ohio. I would like to ask if you have had a case of genuine foot and mouth disease?

Mr. SANDERS. That is a question for a veterinarian to answer, but I will say that we have never had excepting those that have resulted from recent importations, and such as has been directly communicated by them.

Mr. LAWRENCE. It is entirely from imported cattle?

Mr. SANDERS. Yes; we had a cargo arrive in Baltimore last March afflicted with foot and mouth disease in the ship Nessmore. Those cattle were placed in quarantine at once and the disease was stamped out and its spread prevented. But, without proper disinfection this infected ship was loaded with fat cattle at the port of Baltimore and sent back to England. Of course when the ship landed those cattle were found to be suffering from this disease contracted from the infected ship. Another cargo arrived about the same time from Boston under similar circumstances, and the British people at once set up the hue and cry that we were sending them foot and mouth disease from this country; and in July last Mr. Chaplin called attention to this circumstance and introduced a motion, the intent and import of which was to absolutely prohibit the landing of live cattle from this country, because of the alleged prevalence of foot and mouth disease in America. A very thorough investigation by the Treasury Cattle Commission and other veterinarians enabled them to positively contradict that statement. This brought about a very decided change of feeling over there. I was met over there this summer by a strange remark from the American minister when I called upon him to officially assure him that we had no foot and mouth disease in this country. It was a day or two after Mr. Chaplin's motion had passed. When I told him that with the evidence in our possession I felt prepared to state positively that there was no such thing in this country, Mr. Lowell said: "We have told the British people so many lies about the condition of cattle in our country that they will not believe us now that we tell the truth." I will not take up more of your time.

Mr. LAWRENCE, of Ohio. In your opinion, the present precautionary measures are sufficient to protect us against the probability of contagious disease hereafter?

Mr. SANDERS. Not by any means. We have no authority to quarantine sheep, hogs, or goats. The Cattle Commission addressed a letter to the Secretary of the Treasury last September on that very subject, and urged him to direct the collector of each port to cause strict examination of all swine, sheep, &c. And while we have had no authority, our veterinary inspectors have been required to keep watch of the matter, and if they discovered anything in the direction of disease in these animals they have been instructed at once to notify the owners and invoke their assistance in preventing the spread of the affliction. I think this is of very great importance.

Mr. W. T. SMITH, of Iowa. Since arriving in the city I have learned from a gentleman certain facts. He said he had been out at the stock yards talking with a man who had one or two calves from the dairy district from New York to sell. He seemed pretty well posted about a man named Sanders who he said had spent a good deal of money without any return, and had tried very hard to break up this calf trade.

Mr. SANDERS. There is no doubt that this calf trade during the past three years has been the very greatest source of danger to us in the West in bringing the disease from the Eastern States by means of these calves. Many of them have been brought from Ohio and Michigan, which was all right, but as the demand became greater so that calves were brought from further east, the danger increased. Fortunately, or unfortunately, as you have a mind to call it, the men who have bought these calves all over the West have found it a losing business, and in many cases 40 per cent. of calves brought from the East, and sold to the people of the West, have died in less than six months. Thanks to the general warning by the agricultural press and others the people have become very chary of these calves. There is a great danger always from these calves, because it is extremely difficult to tell where they come from.

Mr. BARTLETT, of Illinois. I have made a specialty of handling calves from the East for the last four years, and I have handled a large number of them. I want to say a few words in behalf of the dairy calves. There has been a great deal said in the last two years about the danger we were running in receiving those calves here. I know they are small and weak, and do not seem to have any frames, but I do insist that while for the last twelve years every year we have received in the neighborhood of from 150,000 to 200,000 of these calves shipped from the East to the West, there has not been a case of contagious or infectious disease among one of them. Of course there is a certain rate of mortality among them. The calves are young and tender; but I believe that the highest percentage of loss in any year would not exceed 8 or 10 per cent. Two years ago Governor Cullom issued a proclamation at the request of some of the Short-horn breeders scheduling certain counties, and 1 wrote Governor Cullom that that action was satisfactory to the dairy calf interest for the reason that it defined the region and gave additional assurance to the Western men. I told him that I considered myself fully posted in that business, and I defied any man to show to the contrary. There are conditions regarding the raising of these young calves which all do not understand. It is not profitable to raise calves in certain districts, consequently, in order to ship profitably, they have to be brought and gathered together within a short radius, where they are loaded on cars, and you cannot ship properly unless you get up a car-load, and unless your freights are right. It is not true that the demand is decreasing. I have had an order within the past year for 6,000 head. I can sell 1,000 head to-morrow. I am willing to sell when I can get them for $16 to $18 per head, and I have recently been offered $20, but I can't get them. There has been a vast amount of misrepresentation in this calf trade. The public has become somewhat excited over it and become frightened because they are told they will have pleuro-pneumonia; whereas the harmless creatures are simply doing the best they can to live. [Laughter.] I have seen them come back to the stock yards here as fine stock as you could ask for. I sold 100 head that went into a county in this State three years ago; every one of them lived except three, and two of them were killed in shipment, and the other got into a hay rick. [Laughter.] There has been quite enough of nonsense about this matter. What is the use of talking about the calf trade decreasing when the fact is that we can't get the calves fast enough. I am shipping calves to-day back to Ohio and Virginia. I have just received calves from Chautauqua County, New York, and they were loaded yesterday to go back to West Virginia.

Mr. THOMPSON, of Kentucky. Suppose that to be all true; what assurance have we that infected calves will not be shipped West after all. When prices increase, as they will with this great demand, the disposition to ship will be the greater, and calves will be bought and sold in New York and Pennsylvania, where they have not been sold before. What assurance have we that the danger will not be great in the future, even admitting that it has not been in the past?

Mr. BARTLETT. That might be if your cattle were thoroughbred cattle. That is where this contagious poison is. You never found it in the cattle of commerce.

Mr. W. T. SMITH, of Iowa. I am sorry to learn that the business is profitable. If it was unprofitable the danger would be less; as long as it is profitable the danger is greater. Now, while I am willing to accept this gentleman's statement as true, I am certainly unwilling to believe he is the only gentleman who is shipping calves in this country. Others are in it, and perhaps they too get calves from every infected county, and here, I think, is where we are laboring under very great danger—shipping from the dairy districts in the East to this section. I think, as far as we are concerned, farmers, stockmen, and ranchmen, that we shall do very well to ascertain the history of the calves we buy from the time they were dropped and where they were dropped and who brings them to us.

Professor LAW, of New York. Mr. Chairman, I wish to correct one or two impressions that have doubtless been conveyed. In the first place Mr. Sanders was asked whether foot and mouth disease was ever found among our native cattle. Why, yes. If the question had been asked whether we are ever infected without infection from importations I should say no; a thousand times no. In 1870 it spread from Canada over Northern New York and over the greater part of New England. Dr. Thayer, my colleague on the commission, met me in Albany to consider matters connected with this disease. With regard to the statement that Mr. Bartlett made that we had certain diseases among thoroughbred cattle only, it is utterly pretentious and thoroughly fallacious. Take the poor cattle on the steppes of Eastern Europe and Asia, and we find that we have there the home of the cattle plagues of Europe and Asia. They have the Russian plague there, and it is utter nonsense to talk of its being confined to thoroughbred cattle.

Come to our own country and go south to Texas; there we find our worst indigenous cattle disease. And so we have here shown that the worst cattle of both continents are the subjects of contagious disease. So much for contagious disease belonging to thoroughbred cattle. There has been a reference made to the shipment of calves from Chatauqua County to the West. I happen to live in New York, and in Central New York, and I know a good deal about the state of affairs there. Now, then, a few weeks ago I had a letter from a gentleman in Cayuga County asking if he would be permitted to send two car-loads of calves to his ranch in Nebraska. In my reply I was sorry to have to say "Yes." I know that he was not likely to convey any infectious disease from there to Nebraska, and most certainly he was not likely to convey lung plague But those calves have been received, to my knowledge, not only from Cayuga, but very largely from Chatauqua and other places as far east as Saint Lawrence. One more thing. I would like to say to Mr. Bartlett, in reference to this calf trade, that letters can be produced, I think, from sellers in the Chicago market requesting dealers in the Philadelphia market to send calves to Chicago for sale only.

The PRESIDENT *pro tempore.* The chairman of the committee on order of business has a further report to make.

Mr. C. R. SMITH, of Iowa. We have with us Prof. James D. Hopkins, and also Professor Gadsden. both of whom have brief papers on this subject. We recommend that these papers be presented now.

The recommendation was adopted, and Prof. Jas. D. Hopkins, Territorial veterinarian of Wyoming, addressed the convention as follows :

Prof. HOPKINS. While I was inspector of cattle in New York, I had the good fortune to detect foot-and-mouth disease in a herd that was brought to the port of New York from London on the steamship France. This herd was quarantined, and at the expiration of six months they were turned over to their owners.

Prof. HOPKINS then read the following paper:

The extent to which contagious diseases exist among domestic animals in this country has been fully investigated, and exhaustive reports, accompanied by maps showing the infected localities, have been made by the veterinary division of the Agricultural Department, at Washington, D. C. These reports have been printed by the Commissioner of Agriculture and copies placed in the hands of our legislators, and widely distributed among the people, so that all persons interested in the cattle industry have had abundant opportunities of informing themselves concerning the different diseases our domestic animals may contract by coming in contact with those suffering with a contagious disease, or in journeys through infected roads, pastures, railway cars. or stock yards.

It is not my intention to take up the time of this Convention by going into a detailed description of the various diseases which afflict the domestic animals of the different States, such as anthrax, Texas fever, hog cholera, glanders, and farcy, chicken cholera. or the different diseases of sheep.

The original intention in calling this Convention was to consider the ways and means necessary to secure such legislation as will at an early day remove the restriction placed by the British Government upon our live stock export trade, and also to protect our great western country from an invasion of contagious pleuro-pneumonia among the cattle by stamping it out from where it now exists in the States of New York, New Jersey, Pennsylvania, Maryland, and Virginia.

Pleuro-pneumonia is a highly contagious, febrile disease, peculiar to the ox tribe, having an incubative stage of ten days to three and one-half months, at the end of which local complications arise in the form of extensive inflammatory exudations within the substance of the lung and pleuro, finally resulting in consolidation of some portion of the lungs and adhesion of the pleural surfaces. In some cases there is extensive and rapid destruction of lung tissue with death from suffocation, but most commonly the disease is of a lingering character, symptoms of great prostration manifesting themselves, with blood poisoning from absorption of the degraded pulmonary exudates and death from marasmus.

Contagious pleuro-pneumonia never arises from any condition of keeping or feeding. The disease is *always* introduced into healthful herds through the addition of an animal from an infected locality. Stock yards and railroad cars in an infected district become centers of contagion, and cattle passing through them are exposed to infection. I saw a cow at the Union Stock Yards, New York, suffering with contagious pleuro-pneumonia. This cow was killed by the State authorities. I made the autopsy, and the remainder of the lot, 37 head, were sold to dairymen, thus spreading the contagion, for before leaving New York I was called on to visit three herds, whose owners had bought one each of this infected lot.

Mr. Baldwin, of Paterson, N. J., bought a cow in December, 1881, at the Union Stock Yards, New York, and took her to his farm, where she sickened and died, spreading contagious pleuro-pneumonia to his herd of 34 milch cows, and my last official act in that State was to superintend the destruction and burial of this herd, in April, 1882.

How do stock-yards become infected? Numberless instances are on record where pleuro-pneumonia is known to have broken out in herds whose owners have at once taken them to the yards and placed them on sale, rather than suffer the loss experience taught him was sure to follow.

Again, the pernicious system of cow dealers who peddle cows, exchanging with dairies and returning them to stock yards, often leaving cows on trial at dairies known to be infected, and the cow is afterwards returned to the yards. These men are unscrupulous, and by their peculiar system of trade contagious pleuro-pneumonia is perpetuated and spread among all herds whose owners will trade with them.

It is well known that many people find it profitable to keep cows on the suburbs of cities, where the large open commons furnish free pasturage and the distilleries and starch factories cheap food. These people let their cows run together on the commons, the infected and healthy. They rarely let a fat cow die of this disease, as at the first symptom of illness she is sent to the butcher.

These small herds and their stables are hot-beds of contagion in New York and Brooklyn. Pleuro-pneumonia is the most dangerous of all the cattle plagues, on account of the length of time between exposure to the contagion and development of the disease, during which time the animal presents no abnormal symptom and might be transported to the extreme limits of the country.

In 1882 the Treasury Cattle Commission, after a thorough investigation, made an exhaustive report of the history and spread of contagious pleuro-pneumonia among cattle in this country to the Secretary of the Treasury at Washington, D. C., and pointed out the dread consequences of allowing the disease to spread through the country, and advised the most energetic measures for its eradication. This report was the basis for several bills that were introduced before Congress at its last session. Most unfortunately nothing was done, and our export trade continues to suffer, and the whole country is threatened with an invasion of this terrible pestilence.

Inoculation has been resorted to by the people of Europe, Great Britain, and Australia, which, while it limits the mortality the disease continues to prevail. No country has ever got rid of contagious pluero-pneumonia by inoculation, and to this country, where *so small* a territory is infected in comparison with the vast domain and interests involved, inoculation means perpetuation and spread of the disease. There is only one remedy applicable to this country—*the disease must be stamped out.* If this disease were wide-spread as in England, Europe, or Australia, we would be obliged to resort to inoculation. The work of stamping out pluero-pneumonia from the States where it now exists is an immense undertaking even under the most favorable laws, and requires on the part of those intrusted with the work an extensive knowledge of the rights of individuals, and can be accomplished with very little interference with commerce. It has been demonstrated in Massachusetts, New York, and Connecticut, also in different parts of Europe, that the stamping out of this disease is the *only* effectual remedy. Eminent statesmen who have given this subject close attention cannot agree as to the constitutionality of any law of Congress giving authority to enter a State and prescribe rules and regulations governing the cattle traffic necessary to the slaughter of infected stock ; in other words, "The sovereignty of States must be respected."

If Congress *cannot* enact laws to stamp out contagion, then perhaps Congress *can* enact laws to keep it where it is. Therefore I would propose for your consideration that this Convention shall petition Congress to enact such laws that the Secretary of the Treasury shall appoint a commission of three or five, with authority to prohibit cattle leaving county or counties in any State where contagious pleuro-pneumonia among the cattle exists, except under special license. To prescribe the route all "through cattle" must take in passing the infected district. To investigate all outbreaks of disease among cattle that may become epizootic, and have charge of the quarantine stations for imported cattle. To advise with State authorities as to the best methods of controlling contagious pleuro-pneumonia. To make it a misdemeanor for any one to violate the proclamation of the commission.

If such a commission were appointed, the country would, in a measure, be relieved of its dread of the fatal contagion. But we can never breathe entirely free, while we know that we harbor such an insiduous enemy to our live stock industry.

To make this commission successful, their work must be continuous. Hence an abundant appropriation that will last until the next meeting of the Congress is a necessity.

The moral effect of Federal prohibition on the movement of cattle *from* the infected States, would speedily result in the enactment of the necessary State laws and the stamping out of the contagion.

It is a lamentable fact that with the exception of Illinois and Wyoming Territory the different States pay no attention to the welfare of their live-stock industry. A few of the States have enacted laws against the introduction of pleuro-pneumonia, but they remain a dead letter on the statute-book, for there is no provision made for their enforcement, and in the event of an outbreak of disease among the domestic animals they have no expert at hand to prevent the spread, and also much unnecessary loss among the people. Numerous instances have occurred during the past two years, where the injudicious handling of Southern cattle and Western hogs has spread Texas fever and hog cholera among the Northern and Eastern stock. Again, many animals perish annually, from anthrax, all over the country. Glanders and farcy among horses is a source of heavy loss. These and other diseases indigenous to our country should be a matter for the careful consideration of legislatures of every State and Territory. Therefore, I propose for your consideration that the legislature of every State and Territory shall be petitioned to enact such laws, giving the governor power to appoint a veterinary surgeon, whose duty shall be to investigate all outbreaks of disease among domestic animals, and upon the introduction of any contagious disease the governor shall have authority to quarantine any premises, farms, county, or counties where such disease may exist, and to prescribe such regulations as he may judge necessary to prevent contagion being communicated in any way from the places so quarantined : to call on all sheriffs and deputy sheriffs and police to enforce such rules and regulations ; to prescribe regulations and order the destruction of all animals affected with contagious disease, and for the proper disposition of their hides and carcases, and thorough disinfection of all objects which might convey contagion ; that the owners of all animals so condemned shall be indemnified at least two-thirds sound value ; that all persons transgressing any order of the governor shall be guilty of a misdemeanor ; that a sufficient amount shall be appropriated to enable the governor to enforce the law.

In the stamping out of a contagious disease I am in favor of a liberal indemnity being paid to owners of all condemned animals as the most economical and successful plan, because it secures the owner's hearty co-operation, and in large cities the Government must outbid the dealer and butcher. Then, again, by inducing the people to promptly report all sick cattle, it saves the most expensive professional supervision, and makes the work popular.

Existing legislation, either State or Federal, does not control the movement of cattle. For instance, we have United States quarantine stations in which all cattle from Europe must undergo 90 days' detention on their arrival, while from the hot-beds of contagion around New York and Brooklyn, Philadelphia, or Baltimore, cattle can be transported without let or hindrance to any part of the United States except Illinois and Wyoming Territory.

Heretofore the tide of cattle traffic has been *from* the West, and to this fact we are indebted that contagious pleuro-pneumonia has not spread over the whole country, but at present the great demand for young stock for the Western ranches, makes it an object for the trader to bring cattle from long distances, and unless prohibitive measures are adopted, we will soon see the cheap calves from the infected States brought West to develop pleuro-pneumonia.

Our only safety lies in Congress enacting such laws as will place the prevention of the spread of this pestilence in competent hands, and to insure a continued prosperity it is a matter of necessity that each State shall have a veterinary department ready at all times to cope with any contagion that may be imported, and prevent the consternation and loss to the people consequent on the outbreak of disease among domestic animals.

How this shall be done is a matter for the consideration of this Convention.

Dr. GADSDEN, of Pennsylvania. I would like to say one word in reply to an assertion that some gentleman made, that at the present time England was full of pleuro-pneumonia. Here is an official report—official because it comes from the privy council. It says:

During the five weeks ending September 29, 1883, there were reported in Great Britain thirty-four outbreaks of pleuro-pneumonia and 90 cattle attacked. In the corresponding period of 1882, there were thirty-nine outbreaks, and 104 cattle attacked were reported.''

This I am satisfied is true ; and to let such an assertion go uncontradicted is not right.

Mr. CRANE, of New Jersey. I have lived in the midst of pleuro-pneumonia for twenty years. New Jersey was inoculated from that cow that was sold in Brooklyn to which Professor Law referred this morning, and it was introduced by selling calves from New York State. A friend of mine bought something like 100 of them, sold some to his neighbors, and took the rest to a pasture field in Morris County about 25 miles west. There the disease broke out, and all those calves that were distributed among these neighbors of his carried the disease with them. That was about twenty-five years ago, and there were efforts made to stamp it out, and I think it was pretty thorough, although we were troubled with it several years. About eight or nine years ago it was introduced into Newark, Jersey City, and Elizabeth, by cattle bought in Baltimore by these cow dealers. They could go there and buy cattle for from $10 to $15. Some of them showed signs of the disease. Those that had no signs were distributed among farmers, and the consequence was the disease was sown broadcast in four or five counties. This came to my knowledge and I felt it my duty to take action immediately. I went to the State board of health and stated what was going on, and from there we went to the legislature, and got it to enact laws, similar to those in Massachusetts, to stamp it out. The bill met with a good deal of opposition, especially among those who were afraid to make any appropriation for the purpose through fear their constituents would find fault. We had to labor three years before we got a law, and all this time it was being spread. Some had tried vaccination, but the relief seemed to be only temporary. About the time that Professor Law was attempting to find the disease in New York State the legislature made an appropriation of some $25,000, I think, and gave certain powers to Governor McClellan. He appointed General Sterling from my county, who pursued this thing pretty thoroughly, until the next meeting of the legislature. He had put a pretty effective stop to it by this vaccination and other means, until the State was comparatively quite free from it, and if we had only continued in that way for a year or two longer I think we would have stamped it out entirely. But of course there must be a change, and the matter is now in the hands of the State board of health, and Dr. Hunt is at the head of it; and at the last meeting he reported that there was but a single case, which I think came from Staten Island, New York. I have labored hard, with other gentlemen, before the legislature, to create a popular opinion against this state of things. We believe that our State should have more effectual laws of some kind, and that the board of health or some other organization should have power to stamp this disease out entirely and effectually. I believe that there is not nearly so much now as there was seven or eight years ago.

A DELEGATE. I move that we now adjourn until 9 o'clock p. m. The motion was agreed to; and at 6 o'clock and 47 minutes p. m., the Convention adjourned.

The Convention met at 9 o'clock. the president in the chair.

The PRESIDENT. I understand that in accordance with the report of the committee on order of business, adopted before we adjourned, the first business in order is the reading of a paper by Dr. Gadsden, of Pennsylvania.

Dr. GADSDEN. Before reading my paper, Mr. Chairman and gentlemen, I would like to read a very short paper about New Jersey. A gentleman speaking of New Jersey said there was no disease. or none to speak of there. I allude particularly to pleuro-pneumonia. Two inspectors under the State board of health called at my house on Saturday last and from them I gathered this information:

There are five herds of cattle in quarantine with contagious pleuro-pneumonia. The animals number about 1,200 head. The number that have died in each herd is as follows: 22, 8, 10, 9, 5, in all 54. All the remainder are inoculated with virus from one of the first attacked. None of them have since died, but they have shown symptoms of contagious pleuro-pneumonia in a mild form, but every animal (cattle) brought into these herds of inoculated cattle (if not previously inoculated) have taken contagious pleuro-pneumonia and died or have been killed. They assert and say it can be proved that these cattle took this disease from a lot of 13 that was purchased in March last from a car-load of cattle at Flemington, N. J. They had just arrived from Bradford County, Pennsylvania. The disease was noticed in April last. Ten were put on one farm, 3 on another (this original 13), both belonging to one party. Contagious pleuro-pneumonia broke out on both farms about the same time, 8 out of the 10 died, 1 of the 3 died, another was killed for virus to inoculate the rest, which are doing well. If this report is strictly true it goes a long way to show that inoculated cattle can spread this disease to other cattle coming in contact with them. This is very important, and goes to prove inoculation will not save our herds unless it is possible to inoculate them all, which, of course, is quite out of the question.

Mr. CRANE, of New Jersey. I would state that my authority was from Dr. Hunt.

Dr. GADSDEN. I know Dr. Miller and Dr. Rogers, and I believe every word of that is strictly true.

Mr. CRANE. I would state that I have been over New Jersey since June, and——

Dr. GADSDEN. I would here state that this herd was unknown to Dr. Hunt and Dr. Rogers last July. It was kept from the State authorities. Rather than to report it they thought proper to inoculate.

Professor LAW, of New York. Please tell us where Bradford County, Pennsylvania, is.

Dr. GADSDEN. Two hundred miles from Philadelphia, northwest.

Professor LAW. In the oil regions?

Dr. GADSDEN. I don't know; I haven't been there.

Professor LAW. West of the Alleghanies?

Mr. GADSDEN. It is close to them.

Professor LAW. I merely put the inquiry to show that the source is not to be relied upon.

Dr. GADSDEN. But the man who sold the 13 head says he is sure they came from Bradford County.

Dr. Gadsden then read the following paper:

CONTAGIOUS DISEASES IN CATTLE, HOW THEY ARE IMPORTED, AND WHAT THEY COST.

There are three contagious diseases peculiarly affecting the bovine race, viz., rinderpest or cattle plague, contagious pleuro-pneumonia or lung plague, and sore foot and mouth disease; and the rapidity with which they spread, and the ease with which contagion is communicated, require the adoption of the most stringent measures to eradicate them where they now exist and prevent their further introduction.

None of these plagues are indigenous to this country, but in every instance where they have appeared here the disease can be traced to infected animals that have been imported from Europe.

Fortunately the first named has never made its appearance in this country, although several European nations have suffered terribly by its ravages, and some are still suffering from it.

So far as known it is incurable, and the only remedy is to guard carefully against its introduction by the enforcement of a strict embargo against all countries where it appears, and should it ever obtain lodgment here, adopt the most heroic measures to stamp it out at once. To give some idea of the rapid spread of rinderpest, and the immense loss caused by it, statistics gathered from official sources show that in 1865 and 1866 the loss from it in Great Britain was £12,000,000 or $60,000,000, while in European Russia during the last four years over 1,000,000 cattle have perished with it.

Contagious pleuro-pneumonia or lung plague has made its appearance at different times in this country, and efforts have been made by individual States to stamp it out. In this they have been successful for a time, and at comparatively small cost, but unfortunately only to be again infected from neighboring States that had taken no measures for the prevention of the spread of contagion.

This disease has been known and dreaded in England for many years, and Dr. Fleming asserts that for the six years ending with 1860 more than 1,000,000 cattle perished from it, involving a loss of £12,000,000.

Some persons have denied the identity of the disease that has appeared here, with the scourge of the same name that caused such great loss in England, but having been an inspector in that country for a considerable time, and examined many diseased animals, and made numerous post-mortem examinations, and having had unusual facilities in this country to inspect both living and dead animals affected with the disease, I have no hesitation in pronouncing it *exactly the same disease* as is known as *Pleuro-pneumonia* in England, and of its *contagious* character there can be no doubt.

There have been occasional outbreaks of sore-foot and mouth disease in this country, always traceable to animals brought from Europe, but by the establishment of proper quarantine regulations it has been stamped out without extending to any great extent.

Although this disease readily yields to treatment, it has been productive of great losses in other countries, not only among cattle but also has been communicated to swine and sheep.

In 1871 there were 519,523 animals attacked with it in Great Britain; in 1872 the loss from it in England and Scotland was estimated at £13,000,000, and in 1875 at over £8,000,000. In August of the present year 30,985 animals were attacked with it, and in September only six counties in all England were exempt from its ravages.

Great Britain has adopted the most stringent laws, which are rigidly enforced, to prevent the introduction and spread of contagious diseases among her animals, going so far as to exclude the importation of live animals from countries that have any disease.

This is not to be wondered at, when it is known that from 1839 to 1870 the loss in animals affected with contagious diseases amounted to the enormous sum of £100,000,000 or $500,000,000.

It is a matter of vital importance to this country to promptly take the necessary steps to prevent the importation and spread of these diseases, not only to protect our own food supply, but to prevent the total extinction of our trade in beef with foreign countries.

When we take into consideration the losses sustained by England from these diseases and know that we have five times as many cattle in this country as they have, some idea may be had of the loss we should suffer if these diseases obtained a lodgment here.

If they were once communicated to the vast herds on our western plains, the extirpation of the disease would be next to impossible and the loss which would ensue would be almost incalculable.

The question then arises how are we to prevent so dire a calamity befalling us, for these diseases being purely *contagious*, certainly are *preventable*.

The legislation to effect this object must be *national* in character, and its execution be under the control of the National Government, for if placed in the charge of local authorities, it must prove futile for two reasons: First, on account of favoritism that will naturally be shown to the owners of animals by local officers; and secondly, on account of the failure of certain localities to enact and enforce laws.

There should be restrictions placed on the importation of all animals, animal products, and goods that have been in contact with animals from countries where disease is known to exist, and no animal should be permitted to enter the country until after having been placed in quarantine for a sufficient time to positively determine that it was perfectly free from disease, either in an incipient or active stage.

The Treasury Cattle Commission, to be sure, are taking certain preventive measures in the quarantine of cattle, but it is not thorough, and therefore it does not protect our country. For instance, we have a port at Philadelphia, but we have no quarantine station there, and these animals can come in there and be sent to all quarters of this vast country and these gentlemen know nothing about it.

Secondly. Arrangements should be made for the reception of reports from all sections of the country at short intervals, and upon the appearance or suspicion of disease an inspection should be made by some person competent to detect it; all diseased animals and those that have been in contact with them placed in quarantine, and those without doubt affected with rinderpest or pleuro-pneumonia destroyed as speedily as possible and properly buried. The stables and other out-buildings that have been occupied by these animals should be thoroughly disinfected, and the quarantine maintained for at least three months after the disappearance of the last vestige of the disease.

In the mean time careful inspection should be made from time to time of all animals in the neighborhood.

Animals that are killed should be paid for at a fair valuation, and thus the farmer will have no motive to conceal the appearance of disease for the purpose of saving his stock.

When I speak of quarantine I mean a *complete isolation* of the animals from all others at some place remote from public roads, where they can by no possibility come in contact with any other animals.

By adopting regulations of this character, and having them rigidly enforced by competent officials, under the supervision of some Department of the National Government that shall have the authority to destroy diseased animals and an appropriation to pay for them, such contagious diseases as at present exist can be eradicated from this country and their introduction in the future prevented.

In this way, and in this way alone, can we prevent our vast Western herds from being infected and swept away, and restore to our Eastern seaports and Western cattle markets the trade of which they are now deprived by the English embargo, while the expense to the National Treasury will be trifling in comparison to the results attained.

There has been a further outbreak in Pennsylvania lately. I wish Thomas J. Edge was present, for he could give you not only the particulars of this but every other case they have had. The origin of this case rests with the sale in Baltimore of 16 calves. They were sold in July, and in six weeks the disease broke out. A local farrier, who is also a blacksmith, I believe, made an examination and said he would soon rectify that. Well, he did rectify it, and three of them died. Then the owner wrote to Mr. Edge. They soon found that they were affected. The State has paid $1,200 already for dead animals, and it is expected that it will cost $3,000 before they are through with it, and all on account of this man bringing 16 animals in there last July.

Professor LAW. I beg one word on the subject of Philadelphia. We did not establish a quarantine station there because we were told that Philadelphia steamships would not carry cattle, except under circumstances which were not at all likely to happen, and, therefore, a quarantine station would not be necessary. There is in force an order that all cattle should go to ports where a quarantine station has been established. Now, I learn that they have been coming to Philadelphia, but we are not responsible for it. Moreover, we are not an executive body, but purely advisory. We can advise the Secretary of the Treasury, and there our power ends. We can do nothing else.

The PRESIDENT. Is it the duty of the revenue officer to remand those cattle back to the ship so they can land only at those points where there are quarantine regulations? .

Professor LAW. The duty is to have them sent to the next port where there is a quarantine station.

The PRESIDENT. I understand the next paper is one by Mr. Coffin, of Iowa.

A DELEGATE. Mr. President, we have been listening to a good many papers, and it seems to me that we had better begin to think about taking some action now.

Mr. COFFIN. I have but a very crude paper, which I prepared on my way here. It is simply suggestive of some action, and perhaps the points have been covered by the papers already read. I hardly think it would be profitable to take up the time of the Convention with it.

The PRESIDENT. I presume the Convention would be glad to hear from Mr. Coffin. I was simply reporting to you the action of the Convention. According to the report of the committee Mr. Coffin was to have the floor following the reading of the paper of Dr. Gadsden.

There were several calls for Mr. Coffin, who came forward and presented the following paper:

The vastness of the interests here to be discussed is so beyond all grasp, it is useless to attempt to represent it in figures. Sufficient is it to say that no other one interest touches so many of the citizens of this nation. Now, when we look at the almost entire absence of all authoritative regulation by either the State or national power to protect this interest from danger, as well as the very poverty of the encouragement given for its better development, and of more general scientific and practical knowledge of its propagation and care and feeding, we may well stand filled with wonder and amazement at this lack of attention. Why this is so it is hard at this time to explain. I look upon the fact of this Convention as a most encouraging and auspicious move. Gathered here are representative men from all the stock-raising States and Territories of this nation. The eyes of the law-making powers of the country will be upon us. What this Convention may utter, will, to a large extent, be taken as authority of what is actually needed. Hence, then, I feel very anxious that the deliberations here should be of the most calm, and at the same time far-reaching and exhaustive. As already said, the interest here represented is vastly important. At this present time the money value of the live stock of this nation runs up into figures too great to be well held in the human comprehension, and yet, great as it is, in the very near future it is to be increased to a wonderful degree. When one recognizes the fact as to the great numbers of live stock that are now annually brought to our shores, and the value of each individual one, and at the same time keep in mind that each one of these imported animals is brought here for breeding purposes, and then takes into the account the millions already here which are used also for increasing the number, as well as the individual value of each added one, it does seem that the duty of a wise and thoughtful law-maker should be plain.

What then are the demands now pressing, and what this Convention should with no uncertain sound announce as demanding the immediate attention of the national and State legislatures?

(1.) Immediate steps to secure whatever other precautions that may be necessary to make it absolutely certain that no contagious disease of any kind be ever imported and lodged upon our shores.

(2.) Such laws enacted and powers granted that can effectually and forever stamp out at once whatever there is of contagious diseases among our live stock at the present time. I mean everything the words I use on this last item can bear.

(3.) Under this head, the wants I design to mention may lead to a wide range of thought and discussion.

We as a nation, in comparison to what is done by many other governments to foster and encourage live-stock interest, are doing scarcely anything.

Bear with me for a little while I present this matter as it lies in my own mind. As a nation we are growing rapidly rich. We are soon to be, if our resources are wisely managed, one of the wealthiest peoples of the globe. Our revenues are to be enormous; our national debt is soon to be paid off; already is it a perplexing question with our statesmen what to do with our revenue. Is it not time that Congress should show its appreciation of that interest that lies at the very bottom of all our wonderful prosperity by turning some of this overflowing income that is well nigh bursting our Treasury and corrupting our officials into channels that will establish valuable experimental stations in every State, presided over by experienced and careful men, who will be able in a short time to give valuable information to all the agricultural interests of this land. As it is now we are, in almost every State, left entirely without protection and information.

Let the lung plague break out in almost any of our Western States and we have no law, we have no State officer who has any power to act; we have no expert who can be called upon to decide on the character of the disease. We are all at sea. We have no standard or any fountain, no head center of information to which we can look for real, certain, scientific truth on any of these matters. I do not wish to be understood that I am in favor of any objectionable centralization of power, but I do want a plan by which a man or men whose business it would be to become experts in all these matters, no matter if to arrive at this expertness they shall have learned a great deal of the common, practical, level-headed farmer, as well as by scientific experimentation. But we want these stations and these men to scatter a more general and exact knowledge on agricultural matters; we want a man on whom the people can call, and whose duty and business it will be to go to any part of the State and examine any cases where dangerous diseases may actually or be supposed to exist.

Is it not time that we moved in this direction of securing to the agricultural interests of the whole nation local experimental stations to foster, encourage, and protect all its interests?

Is not a convention of such men as we have here a proper one to strike boldly out for these things in such a form and manner as its wisdom may dictate? We must remember that public sentiment, that gives birth to and maintains laws that are needed for and in the advancement of a great people's interests, is a matter of growth, and can we afford to neglect the cultivation of that kind of public sentiment that must be before we can reach the end so greatly desired and needed?

A DELEGATE. I should be pleased to ask Professor Law what effect, in his judgment, the milk or flesh from an animal affected with pleuro-pneumonia would have upon the system of man?

Professor LAW. I am sorry to say that it will convey no actual disease to man. I have almost wished it were different, because if it was harmful to man it would be stamped out soon enough. Of course in the advanced stages of the disease the milk, what there is of it, is at least vastly impure, and the system is certainly saturated with obnoxious products; but we cannot trace any definite disease to man from this, other than perhaps a little ill-health. It never produces pleuro-pneumonia in man, or anything akin to it.

[Following this answer there occurred a running coloquy between Professor Law and a delegate, a large portion of which could not be heard at the reporter's table.]

Mr. SCOTT, of Iowa. Mr. Chairman, this Convention is composed of representative men—supposed to be representative men—who are interested in this question, and which was supposed by the Department of Agriculture to be of importance enough to call us together in a national Convention, and the time specified for its consideration was two days. One of those days, if my time be estimated properly and noted, has very nearly expired, and as yet it seems to me we are frittering away the little that is left of this first day in the discussion of some of the details in regard to questions that any one could have settled for themselves by going to some of our libraries or consulting some of the publications that have been sent out gratuitously during the past year. Here for the last ten minutes we have been listening to questions that any of those engaged could have had asked and answered either before or after we met. [Applause.] It seems to me, sir, that if we could rise to the dignity that belongs to a national Convention representing more than 50,000,000 of population and more than $60,000,000,000 of wealth, and more than $15,000,000,000 of annual productions—if we would rise to the dignity which belongs to men who represent interests of such great magnitude, we should address ourselves to the presentation of our views as a Convention, and the only practical manner, sir, that I can conceive of by which that can be done is by the usual method of a deliberative body—the expression of views through formal resolutions. [Applause.]

There are some things that are conceded. We have had the matter discussed to-day, and it is conceded that in a comparatively small portion of this vast country there does exist infectious cattle disease. It is also conceded (probably an important fact to us) that it does occupy but a very small portion of our vast domain. It is further conceded also (and these things might, all of them, be embodied in a formal "whereas") this fact and "whereas" that fact, and "whereas" also this further fact) that it is only because the movement of the live stock of the country has been from the west to the east that we have been saved from a fearful disaster. Figures do not fairly convey to the human mind the terrible importance of this subject to us. No, neither figures nor language will convey it to us; at least I have not sufficient command over the language to represent to this Convention what our vast animal production means to this country, nor what it means should this disease get among our herds and scatter them like leaves before the autumn blast. [Applause.] Now, sir, you suggested in your remarks this morning the time and the means which must be adopted to cause our Government to realize to some extent the precise facts in regard to this matter, and the necessity of prompt action. I am sure we all realize the necessity of using these means and of bringing them to bear upon the Government, and I make these remarks, Mr. President, with the view of calling forth from the committee on resolutions, or from any other source, some sort of action which shall bring us face to face with our duty in this matter before the day is entirely gone. [Applause.] I would ask if the committee on resolutions, or order of business, or any authority of the officers of this Convention, is prepared to present to this Convention any formal resolution through which this body can express itself only as a deliberative body can. [Applause.]

The PRESIDENT. There were several committees appointed, but I am not informed that either is ready to report at this time.

Mr. SCOTT. I trust we shall have something placed before this Convention at once that means action and business. [Applause.]

The PRESIDENT. Will the gentlemen make a motion to that effect?

A DELEGATE: We know that a large amount of money has been expended and a great deal of effort undertaken, and yet contagious lung plague still exists in this country. Now I think that the reason for that may be explained by the fact that the institutions of this country differ from those of other countries in which such organizations exist. Here in this country we have gone into some States and seen the plague extirpated from them, while in other States the disease has been quite prevalent, and little or no attempt made to stamp it out there. The question arises what practical method shall we adopt to eradicate this disease, and that question can be answered only in one way—there must be combined action on the part of the Federal Government and the State government. This has already been alluded to by Professor Law, but in any attempt which shall be made to eradicate this disease the Federal Government must make a sufficient appropriation to carry on the work, and then the different States must adopt a uniform legislation, so that all States which are infected will take a united and harmonious action. Then we shall not have the spectacle of one State being free of the disease while another is still suffering from it. We can incorporate these principles in any resolution that may be brought before us. We must follow the principle of action by the Federal Government; and we must adopt, to a certain extent, the principle of the Government supervising the State action, but we cannot relegate the entire duty to the Federal Government; it must to a certain extent be carried out by the different States. I think that by recognizing these two principles that we may ultimately see this country entirely free from the lung plague, and I think that in any resolution which is to be adopted by the Convention it will be well to limit our action to one disease. That is enough to grapple with at one time; and when we have seen the country rid of lung plague it will then be time for subsequent efforts to remove those other diseases which also inflict considerable loss upon us.

Professor MORROW. I heartily appreciate the force of the remarks made by my friend, Mr. Scott, of Iowa. I have also felt that the time had come when we should endeavor to get formal action before the Convention. As a means of securing this I would move that the committee on resolutions be requested to report to this Convention at the earliest practical moment a plan for our consideration and action.

The PRESIDENT. If any gentleman has a plan or resolution to offer let it be referred to this committee, in order that it may consider all suggestions together.

A DELEGATE. I suggest that the names of that committee be read.

The secretary read the list of names.

The DELEGATE from Wyoming. I am a very young man to even attempt to make a speech in a convention of this kind; but I do want to say that I hardly think the vast interests here are properly represented upon that committee. The delegation of which I am a part has come here from a long distance. That delegation represents on this floor from twelve to twenty millions of dollars invested on the plains, and I beg that we may have a representation upon that committee, and that the name of our president, Judge James Carey, be added to that committee. I think that his advice will be of great help.

The name of Mr. Carey was accordingly added to the committee.

Mr. POST, of Illinois. I would suggest that inasmuch as there may be those present who have prepared resolutions, or formulated some action for the Convention, that the roll be called for the purpose of allowing every one present to offer any such suggestion, and they be referred to the committee without debate. I make this suggestion in order that we may get some idea of the plan of operation that members have in mind. That will suggest other resolutions, and we shall know something of what we have before the Convention.

Mr. SCOTT, of Iowa. There seems to be some absent members of that committee. It appears to me that the number, 5, on so important a committee as this is to be is wholly inadequate to the proper representation of the feelings of our whole extent of country. By reason of this fact I move that the number be increased to 10, and the additional members be selected from those States not already represented upon the committee.

A DELEGATE. Will the gentleman not accept an amendment to make the committee consist of one member from each State represented here?

The amendment was accepted, and the motion, as amended, was adopted.

Mr. SCOTT. I rise to name Mr. Dailey, of Nebraska, as a member of that committee.

Mr. DAILEY, of Nebraska. I should like to present the name from my own State—Mr. S. R. Thompson.

The roll of States was called by the secretary, the nominations received and ratified, as follows:

Wyoming, James Carey; Colorado, George W. Rusk; Pennsylvania, Julius Le Moyne; Michigan, I. H. Butterfield, jr.; Arizona, J. J. Gosper; Wisconsin, Hiram Smith; Minnesota, George E. Case; West Virginia, J. M. Kirk; Nebraska, Prof. S. R. Thompson; Tennessee, Col. John Overton; Maryland. Edward B. Emory; District of Columbia, Dr. D. E. Salmon; Massachusetts, Dr. E. F. Thayer; Kansas, Governor Dick; Iowa, Hon. John Scott.

The committee thereupon retired, and, on motion, the Convention adjourned at 10 o'clock until 8 a. m. to-morrow.

NOVEMBER 16.

The Convention awaited the report of the committee on resolutions until 9 o'clock and 40 minutes, when it was called to order by the president.

Mr. CHORN, from the committee, said: With your permission, sir, the committee on resolutions is ready to report, and the secretary will read our report.

(The report was read. It appears hereafter in sections and in its amended form.—REPORTER.)

Mr. SANDERS, of Illinois. I move the adoption of the report.

Professor HOPKINS, of Wyoming. I notice that the first portion of the preamble refers to the matter as "disease among domestic animals." I would suggest that the disease be distinctly named. I believe that it will be better if we confine our influence to the one disease of contagious pleuro-pneumonia.

Mr. THOMPSON, of Nebraska. Mr. President, this matter was very fully discussed by the committee. This Convention was called, as we understand, to consider what measures are necessary to stamp out all classes of disease among domestic animals. The gentlemen who are interested in swine are particularly interested in this question, and we thought our action due to them, while the next portion of the preamble is fully directed toward this one disease of pleuro-pneumonia.

Mr. GRINNELL. I move the adoption of the first portion, and the amendments can come up in order.

A DELEGATE. I rise to make a motion that each speaker upon the report and amendments be confined to ten minutes.

(Suggestions of five minutes were heard from all parts of the room.)

The amendment was accepted, and the motion, as amended, was agreed to.

Professor LAW. I now call for the reading of the first " whereas."

The secretary read as follows:

Whereas the existence of disease among animals in the United States has seriously affected the exportation of live stock, and the suspicion that attaches in foreign countries to all neat cattle and swine of the United States on account of the existence of disease in certain localities, has greatly lessened the sale of American meats in foreign markets.

This portion of the preamble was then adopted.

The secretary then read the second portion of the preamble as recommended by the committee, as follows:

And whereas the existence of pleuro-pneumonia in certain of the Atlantic States, introduced from time to time by the importation of live stock from European countries, constantly threatens the spread of the contagion to the Southern and Western States and Territories; that the disease is of such a character that State legislation can only give partial relief; that prompt and appropriate legislation on the part of Congress to eradicate the disease is imperatively demanded; that should the great ranges of the West become infected with the disease it would be impossible to stamp out the plague except by the total destruction of the herds, and at a cost of hundreds of millions of dollars.

Professor ROBERTS, of New York. If I quote it properly, that portion reads, " In certain Atlantic States" the disease prevails. I want to suggest that it be amended to read in " certain portions of the Atlantic States." As it is now, it is too sweeping. It conveys the impression that the disease exists all through certain Atlantic States, when the truth is, it is confined to small portions of a few of those States. I move that the words "small portions" be inserted.

Professor HOPKINS, of Wyoming. I think it would be better to name the States where the disease exists, as the locality is well known all over the world. Why should we brand the whole Atlantic coast with the stigma of the disease when everybody knows that it is only certain States that have it? Why not name the States?

Mr. EMORY, of Maryland. I do not think it would be possible to name the States, because the disease is one that fluctuates from time to time. Maryland has been very much affected with pleuro-pneumonia. I don't think there is now one case in the State. We had an outbreak in Washington County a few weeks ago, but the animals were slaughtered and I don't think there is a single case in the State at the present time. I think that a few cases of Texas fever is now quarantined there, but to state that this disease exists there would not be fair. Of course we are liable to the disease there from time to time. It is brought from other States into the Baltimore stock yards. It is liable to be carried through the State by the purchases of feeders from Virginia. The last case of pleuro-pneumonia was from West Virginia. I have been told by our State veterinarian that we have none there now, and to state that it exists there or in Pennsylvania might lead to trouble.

Dr. GADSDEN. With all respect to this committee on resolutions, I do hope that you will stick to this one fatal disease known as pleuro-pneumonia. If you go into swine fever, chicken cholera, and all those other diseases, and everything else that is contagious in this country, I am afraid you will never succeed in getting one dollar from the national Treasury. The expense would be so great as to frighten those gentlemen at Washington. If you are going to render the country a service in your efforts to secure needed legislation, I do hope that you will confine your efforts to one thing at a time. Let that be pleuro-pneumonia, and I trust you will succeed in stamping out this dreaded pest from this country.

Professor LAW. With regard to the remarks of the gentlemen from Maryland (Mr. Emory) I wish to say a word. Now I do not know where this disease exists in Maryland, but I am as confident that it does exist there as I am of my own existence. I don't blame our friends for standing by their State. They don't regret the existence of this plague any more than I do; but I am as confident that it is in Maryland as I am that I am in this room.

Mr. EMORY. We have a regular inspection in Maryland. We have a State veterinarian who visits the stock yards every Monday morning and makes a thorough inspection.

Professor LAW. We had an inspection in New York in 1879, and the officer in charge of it had quite a number of inspectors employed in visiting the dairies constantly. They insisted that I would find no pleuro-pneumonia in the State of New York. Dr. Hopkins and Professor Salmon can tell what they found; we found it everywhere from Water street on the south to Yonkers on the north. These inspections, unless they are thorough, and made for all the herds, and made continually, will miss of finding the disease. Now it is asserted that there is an inspection of the stock yards, but I am as confident that it exists in Baltimore as it is possible to be, and a thorough inspection will show it.

Professor MORROW. I think the remarks to which we are listening illustrate the certainty that if we attempt to specify States we shall get into an interminable debate. There is a natural sensitiveness that States that have it shall not be named, and I therefore move that the second portion of the preamble be amended to read "a small portion of the State of New York."

Professor ROBERTS, of New York. Oh, no; a "very small portion of a few of the Atlantic States."

Mr. CHORN, of Kentucky. The committee are willing to accept that amendment.

Professor HOPKINS. It has been published all over the world in what

State or States it exists, and why should we place the stigma upon all the Atlantic States.

The PRESIDENT. The amendment is made to read "in small portions of a few of the Atlantic States."

Professor HOPKINS. There are 2,000 miles of seaboard, and they should not be made to suffer the stigma when it has been published all over the world by the Treasury Cattle Commission and by the Department of Agriculture that that disease exists in New York, New Jersey, Pennsylvania, Maryland, and Virginia, and why should we say a "few of the Atlantic States." Let us give it where it is known; where the English Government know it exists; where we have had inspectors who have found the disease. In 1879 the English Government sent Professor McEachran to the United States, and his report of finding this disease here was the basis whereby the restrictions upon our live stock were placed. When they know, and when everybody knows, that the stock yards in Baltimore and other cities are infected, let us give the name of the States, let the people know that we know where the disease exists, and that we are determined to do all in our power to stamp it out.

Mr. EMORY. In reference to what I said about the non-infection of the stock yards in Baltimore, I believe, after conversation with Professor Ward before coming here, that the State is free from disease, and at the same time it may be thoroughly impregnated with the disease at any time. It would not, however, be proper to brand us to-day as an infected State. I would not state that the stock yards were never infected. I have reason to believe that the disease is carried there from time to time, but we have a most rigid examination there now, and I believe we are entirely clear.

Professor LAW. How many animals are received at the stock yards daily?

Mr. EMORY. Several thousand.

Professor LAW. And he examines several thousand a day; a pretty good day's work.

Mr. EMORY. Of course he does not examine every individual animal; he visits the yards and looks over the stock. The Live Stock Association of Maryland have taken hold of this question, and they propose to memorialize the legislature this winter to get proper legislation.

A DELEGATE. I move an amendment to the amendment; that we insert the names of the States that have this disease.

Mr. W. T. SMITH, of Iowa. If we enter into these matters of detail we shall not get through in a month. We have attempted to deal in general terms, and have recommended the appointment of a committee whose duty it shall be to state the facts to Congress. I don't think it wise for this Convention to attempt to go into all the details. Leave that to the committee that we have provided for. I simply wish to offer the substance of what Mr. Roberts suggested, that for the words "in certain of the Atlantic States" this portion of the preamble be amended to read "in certain portions of the States on the Atlantic seaboard."

The amendment was agreed to, the previous amendment being understood to have been withdrawn. The second portion of the preamble as amended was then adopted.

The PRESIDENT. The secretary will read the first resolution.

The secretary read as follows:

Resolved, That we urge upon the proper authorities the importance of a thorough inspection of all live stock and meat products shipped to foreign countries.

A DELEGATE. I move its adoption.

Professor LAW. I think in this we are greatly increasing our expenditure without any corresponding benefit. The inspection of our live stock going to foreign countries cannot prevent the exportation of pleuro-pneumonia, nor yet Texas fever, the two great diseases that the English fear. Why should we ask for this examination? All exporters employ veterinarians and have an examination made on their own ground. The ship companies that insure the cattle have an examination on their account. The shipment of cattle suspected of the disease is never thought of, but the disease may remain latent in the system of an animal for at least three months. No inspector can detect that. The Texas fever may remain latent in the system from thirty to sixty days. No inspector can detect that. I propose that this resolution be eliminated as a matter of undue expense at the present time, and as likely to call upon Congress for too much money, and as likely to divert the money into other channels that will not have a correspondingly good effect. I move that this resolution be omitted from the report.

Mr. SANDERS, of Illinois. I am loth to differ with my associate and friend Professor Law upon anything, especially upon matters of this kind, for I acknowledge his very great learning upon every question of this nature; but I do hope that this resolution will be adopted exactly as reported by this committee. Among the very many things discussed by myself and Professor Brown was this question. He said to me explicitly that there was no one movement that this Government could undertake that would go farther toward securing the admission of our cattle there, and removing all restrictions, than an inspection under the sanction of Government. So far as I heard an expression among the American consuls in every city in Germany I visited, and from members of the German Government and people, it was unanimously to the effect that the very moment our Government adopts any sort of inspection they would remove their restriction upon American pork. I admit freely that inspection will not detect certain diseases, but an inspection as against foot and mouth disease and pleuro-pneumonia is not the only thing that we have to think of; they are not the only things that foreigners are afraid of.

Professor LAW. Mr. Sanders said yesterday that Professor Brown said that as long as there was pleuro-pneumonia here, just so long would the Government retain those restrictions. Professor Brown said to me that he fully appreciated the situation, and that as a scientific man he acknowledged the justice of our claims ; but, said he, "What we find when the cattle arrive here is that they have foot and mouth disease." Examination cannot prevent foot and mouth disease, for it is contracted on board ship, and they will show it all the same whether there is an inspection here or not.

Dr. DETMERS, of Illinois. I simply have to say that thorough inspection of all the meat products is an impossibility in our country, as every one will see who is acquainted with the immense quantity of meat product furnished alone by Chicago. For instance, Armour & Company kill 7,000 hogs every day. How many men would it take to inspect that meat? It would be a great expense to our Government, and no Congressman would be willing to vote for such an outlay. It cannot be done.

Mr. SCOTT, of Iowa. I favor the motion as made to strike this out, for the reason that this resolution departs from the objects of this Convention. We have not met here for the purpose of protecting European countries; we have met here for the purpose of inaugurating a movement that shall stamp out the disease in our own country. [Great applause.] If we undertake to do this, that, and the other thing for the purpose of pandering to the interest of exporters, and of those who are carrying on the trade, we shall depart from the objects which have called us here—which, as I understand, is to bring about such measures as shall stamp out this disease. Let us confine ourselves, then, to the business that has brought us together. [Applause.]

Professor HOPKINS, of Wyoming. If it is the object of making an inspection of cattle going to European countries, to give them a clean bill of health, I will say that it is impossible for any veterinarian to de-detect disease by an inspection of cattle going on board. He must know where the cattle come from, and know their history for at least three months. It is impossible to do this thing. I have examined cattle and know all about it, and if at present, in an examination, I could discover no symptom of contagious disease, I would not give a clean bill of health to cattle going on board ship bound for Europe. I have examined thousands going to Europe.

Mr. GRINNELL, of Iowa. I hope, sir, that we will sustain the committee. I believe that resolution is drawn properly. It covers the ground, and in reply to my friend Governor Scott, who says this is not the purpose of this Convention, I want to say that I was sent here to do the very thing that this proposes to do. There is a cloud upon us, and I propose to remove it as far as possible. What are my friends here for from the West—from these ranges where they rear cattle that shall be good beef, above suspicion, to be sent abroad to bring the best prices. If we cannot do all that we profess to do, let us show the world that we are equal to this emergency; let us show to all Europe that there are men here from twenty States, who have come together to ask the national Congress to do all that we could do, to the end that we may send our product abroad with a clean bill of health. I hope, sir, you will pass this resolution as it stands, to show our good intent at least. I think my friend is not exactly right, because we are here, not only to stamp out what we have, but to rectify our reputation. We want to raise our reputation where it has fallen into straits. [Applause.]

Professor LAW. I wish to say this, that if we are to give a certificate of our cattle shipped from New York and Baltimore, on the basis of examination we will simply add one other instance to the other instances already quoted in which we tell them lies.

Dr. GADSDEN, of Pennsylvania. I have the honor of knowing Professor Brown as well as any man in this room. He is the advisor of the privy council, where his advice has great influence, and he assured me last year that as long as we have one case of contagious disease these restrictions will ever be against us. That is the law of their land. They have placed this upon us because of the demand of their people, and you must remove the cause before they will remove the restriction. I went there for the purpose of getting Pennsylvania cattle released from the embargo. They told me that I need not trouble myself, as the law said as long as the disease existed in this country the restriction should be made. Unless we can get rid of this thing, the first thing we know we will have restrictions against receiving our cattle at all. It only wants proper working on the part of members over in Parliament, and if you do get it you will never get it wiped out.

Mr. SANDERS, of Illinois. I don't wish these veterinarians to understand that I make the assertion that Professor Brown told me that if we had an inspection the English Government would remove these restrictions. What he said was that it would be one of the best things we could do, and that we could not do any one thing that would be a greater step in the right direction, but you must stamp out your disease and inspect and keep up your inspection. Now, because we cannot do everything, I don't think any one should say that we ought not to do what we can do. Professor Brown urged me to recommend in my report this very thing, not as *the* one thing, but *one* of the things we could do.

Professor THOMPSON, of Nebraska. As a member of the committee I desire to say to the Convention that one object in recommending this resolution was to show our good intention. We may not be able to induce Congress to appropriate money necessary to appoint inspectors, but let us show to foreigners that we are willing to do the best we can. It was for the good effect, more than anything else, that we recommended this.

There were loud cries for the question, and, upon a division, the motion of Professor Law to strike out the resolution was agreed to—27 to 25.

The secretary then read the second resolution, as follows :

Resolved, That this Convention heartily indorse the action of the Secretary of the Treasury in enforcing quarantine against all infected cattle, for the purpose of preventing the further importation of foreign contagious diseases, and we recommend that the regulations be enforced with rigid impartiality against all importers. And further that Congress should be asked to confer authority upon the Treasury Department to quarantine sheep, swine, and goats.

Mr. CAREY, of Wyoming. I move the adoption of the resolution.

Professor LAW. I object to this on similar grounds to those which actuated me in my motion with reference to the resolution before this. It is going to draw away considerable money for an object that can very well be left. Sheep and swine are not likely to convey disease to us, but at the same time the Treasury has the power to have all sheep and swine examined. So far as foot and mouth disease is concerned we know that it does show on arrival. They take the disease in from twenty-four hours to one week or thereabout. They pass through it on the ship, and in very many cases they are reasonably well over it when they arrive. At the same time the disease leaves such sores that any man who is worthy of his name can detect and will detect it on arrival. I don't know of an instance where a true veterinarian, I don't know of a person who is practicing with a degree who has passed a lot of cattle, sheep, or swine afflicted with disease. At present we have the measures to prevent the importation of this disease. They will not take up pleuro-pneumonia or any of those long-continued diseases. We are not at all likely to import sheep-pox because they haven't it there, and because when they do get it they know precisely where it is. This is going to draw away a deal of money and afford no adequate compensation.

Mr. SANDERS, of Illinois. One word in reference to the reason why that resolution should pass. I drafted that resolution and I insist it should be adopted. There will be no necessity for Congress to compel the Secretary to quarantine all sheep and swine for sixty to ninety days. The object is simply to confer the authority to quarantine, and he can make such regulations in regard to the length or conditions, as Professor Law may advise. There is this difficulty as the matter now stands: When we examin sheep and swine and find them infected with foot and mouth disease or any other disease, the question is, what are you going to do with them? You have no authority in the world to say a thing about it. The owner may say "they are not diseased and I am going to take them home." And there is no law to prevent him. We can issue a circular to collectors of the port asking them to examine imported sheep, swine, and goats; but suppose we find disease, what are we going to do about it ?

Professor LAW. Send it back.

Mr. SANDERS. There is no authority to send it back. All we can say is, "you ought not to take these infected hogs or sheep home." They can say "we don't believe they are infected," and they can take them home and we cannot help it.

A DELEGATE. I move to strike out all reference to sheep, swine, and goats.

The motion was not agreed to.

The question then recurred upon the adoption of the resolution as reported by the committee, and it was agreed to without a division.

The secretary then read the third resolution, as follows:

Resolved, That we recommend that, for the purpose of reaching definite and conclusive action, a committee of five be appointed by the Chairman of the Convention, whose duty it shall be to present a memorial to congress setting forth explicitly the loss and damage we have sustained in our business, not only by reason of the fact that contagious diseases do exist to a limited extent in this country, but also of the much greater loss and damage we sustain by reason of the embarrassing restriction, and, in some cases, prohibitory regulations which have been adopted by foreign Governments against American live stock and their meat products. We further recommend that said committee be instructed to confer with the Secretary of the Treasury, the Commissioner of Agriculture, and such other officials and persons as to them shall be deemed proper, and shall thereafter suggest to Congress such points of legislation as they may deem the best calculated to protect our interests and remove foreign prejudice against our meat productions. We further recommend that all live stock organizations in the United States be invited to co-operate with us by advice, suggestions, and cash subscriptions, to be used in defraying the necessary expenses of said committee; and further, that the said invitation be extended to transportation and stock yard companies, beef and pork packers and exporters, and all others having an interest in common with us in this matter.

Mr. GRINNELL, of Iowa. I move that where the word "five" occurs that the word "nine" be inserted. In the first place a committee of nine people from different sections may better combine and bring together the thoughts of the whole nation than five can; consequently, when we come to act upon Congress we want as many strings as possible. We want all sections, all interests, all parties represented in asking this action of the American Congress. Any gentleman who has been there knows how hard it is to procure legislation. A member of Congress has to do everything, as the president knows, except take in washing [great laughter], and we want a strong committee to induce these people to listen to us and heed our appeal; not a committee to go there simply to sit around and spend their time, but one that will go there and work in season and out of season, composed of those who will go to the houses of these members and meet them in committee and push this matter. My notion is that if this Convention gives each of these Congressmen notice that it is his political death for him to refuse to help us, and that he will lose the votes of his district if he fails to help in the matter, that you will get what you want. [Laughter and applause.] Let them understand that if they don't take care of you you will take care of them [laughter], and if they fail to aid you give them to understand that at the next election they will have need of the services of a political undertaker. [Great laughter.]

7924 C B——5

Professor HOPKINS, of Wyoming. I would rather it would be nineteen, and it would be still better if it were nineteen hundred, and let them take Congress by storm.

The amendment of Mr. Grinnell was adopted.

The PRESIDENT. The Chair is not well enough informed to appoint this committee, and the best way to have it done is for the delegations to suggest one or two men from those States who are likely to be willing to act for us in this matter. I don't know the delegates well enough myself: I want to choose the very best men we have. I want the help of every one of you when I get there this winter. We want no drones there.

The resolution as amended was then agreed to.

Mr. STURGIS, of Wyoming. I wanted to make a motion to amend before the resolution was adopted. It would have been to this effect:, That this committee shall consist of one member from each State and Territory represented here instead of the nine members provided for. Each State could name its member upon the roll call, and in my judgment we should then have an effective and representative committee.

A DELEGATE. I move a reconsideration of the last vote by which we adopted the resolution, with a view to amending the resolution as suggested by the secretary.

The motion to reconsider was agreed to.

The DELEGATE. I now move that the word "nine" be stricken out and that there be inserted "one member from each State and Territory represented."

The amendment was agreed to; and the resolution as amended was then adopted.

The secretary proceeded to call the roll of States.

Mr. COFFIN, of Iowa. Would it not be well to give time for each delegation to confer before they nominate their member of this committee?

Mr. SANDERS. I suggest, Mr. Chairman, that we all proceed to that without further formality. It is not essential that this committee should be announced at this meeting. The delegations can take their time to consult in order to select their best and strongest man.

The PRESIDENT. I think it is best to have the committee announced before we adjourn *sine die.*

A DELEGATE. I suggest that it will be well for us to dispose of this report of the committee before we take up any other business.

The PRESIDENT. The secretary will read the remainder of the report.

The secretary read as follows:

Resolved, That the thanks of this Convention are due to the Hon. George B. Loring, Commissioner of Agriculture, for the hearty and efficient manner in which he has co-operated with the live-stock breeders of the United States, and the efficient aid he has given us: and that the President of this Convention be requested to invite him to act as *ex officio* chairman of the committee which shall be appointed in accordance with the foregoing resolution.

The resolution was unanimously agreed to.

The full text of the preamble and resolutions adopted is as follows:

Whereas the existence of disease among domestic animals in the United States has seriously affected the exportation of live stock, and that the suspicion that attaches in foreign countries to all neat cattle and swine of the United States on account of the existence of diseases in certain localities has greatly lessened the sale of American meats in foreign markets; and

Whereas the existence of pleuro-pneumonia in certain portions of the States on the Atlantic sea-board introduced from time to time by the importation of live stock from European countries, constantly threatens the spread of the contagion to the Southern and Western States and Territories, and the disease is of such a character that State legislation can only give partial relief; and since prompt and appropriate legislation on the part of Congress to eradicate the disease in the infected districts is imperatively demanded; and since, should the great ranges of the West become infected with the disease, it would be impossible to stamp out the plague except by the total destruction of the herds, and at a cost of hundreds of millions of dollars: Therefore,

Resolved, That this Convention heartily indorse the action of the Secretary of the Treasury in enforcing quarantine against all imported cattle for the purpose of preventing the further importation of foreign contagious diseases, and we recommend that the regulations be enforced with rigid impartiality against all importers. And, further, that Congress should be asked to confer authority upon the Treasury Department to quarantine infected sheep, swine, and goats.

Resolved, That we recommend that, for the purpose of reaching definite and conclusive action, a committee to consist of one member from each State and Territory represented, be appointed by the chairman of this Convention, whose duty it shall be to present a memorial to Congress setting forth explicitly the loss and damage we have sustained in our business, not only by reason of the fact that contagious diseases do exist to a limited extent in this country, but also of the much greater loss and damage we sustain by reason of the embarrassing restriction, and in some cases prohibitory regulations, which have been adopted by foreign Governments against American live-stock and dead-meat products. We further recommend that said committee be instructed to confer with the Secretary of the Treasury, the Commissioner of Agriculture, and such other officials and persons as to them shall be deemed proper, and shall thereafter suggest to Congress such points of legislation as they may deem the best calculated to protect our interests and remove foreign prejudice against our meat productions. We further recommend that all live-stock organizations in the United States be invited to co-operate with us by advice, suggestions, and cash subscriptions to be made in defraying the necessary expenses of said committee, and, further, that the said invitation be extended to transportation and stock-yard companies, beef and pork packers, and exporters, and all others having an interest in common with us in this matter.

Resolved, That the thanks of this Convention are due to Hon George B. Loring for the hearty and efficient manner in which he has co-operated with the live-stock breeders of the United States, and the efficient aid he has given us, and that the president of this Convention be requested to invite him to act as *ex officio* chairman of the committee which shall be appointed in accordance with the foregoing resolutions.

Mr. W. T. SMITH, of Iowa. Before we adjourn, sir, representing the State of Iowa, which has more cattle than any State in this country except Texas, and more cattle than a half dozen Territories, I rise to say that our delegation has agreed upon the name of the Hon. J. B. Grinnell, ex-member of Congress, to represent Iowa upon this commit. tee. [Applause.]

Mr. GOSPER, of Arizona. I rise pleasantly to ask the president of
the Wyoming Cattle Association how many cattle they have in the
Territory as compared with Iowa. There seems to be a disposition,
perhaps, not exactly to ignore the fact that the great plains are alive
with cattle, but there seems to be an ignorance on the part of some in
relation to this matter. The Western men are more alive to this matter because they have so much more at stake.

Mr. W. T. SMITH, of Iowa. Well, I have owned cattle in Wyoming and
Iowa. I may say to my friend from Arizona (Mr. Gosper) that Iowa
contains, according to the last census, more than Nebraska, Wyoming,
California, Utah, Colorada, Nevada——

Mr. GOSPER. Hold on; that is enough. [Great laughter.]

Mr. GRINNELL, of Iowa. I would like to say that it cost me $100
to get that information in advance. I shall not ask to have a contribution to remunerate me for the information, but the gentleman states a
fact. [Laughter.]

Mr. CAREY, of Wyoming. I would like to ask the gentleman what
census he refers to.

Mr. W. T. SMITH, of Iowa. To 1880.

Mr. CAREY, of Wyoming. I would like to inform the gentleman that
he could not go to-day where the cattle roam in Wyoming, and buy them
for $100,000,000, and he must remember that what has been done there
has been done almost entirely since General Crook took possession there
in 1876. [Applause.]

A DELEGATE. I move a recess for fifteen minutes, for the purpose of
enabling the delegates to confer upon nominations for this committee.

The motion was agreed to.

Upon reassembling the secretary proceeded to call the roll of States
Territories, and the following nominations for membership upon the committee were ratified by the Convention:

Wyoming.—Hon. J. M. Carey, Cheyenne.
Ohio.—Hon. Columbus Delano, Mount Vernon.
Colorado.—Hon. William J. Wilson, Denver.
New York.—Col. N. M. Curtis, Ogdensburg, N. Y.
Illinois.—Hon. D. W. Smith, Bates.
Pennsylvania.—Julius LeMoyne, Washington.
Iowa.—Hon. J. B. Grinnell, Grinnell.
Kentucky.—T. C. Anderson, Mount Sterling.
Texas.—Hon. George B. Loving.
Arizona.—J. J. Gosper.
Wisconsin.—Hon. Hiram Smith, Sheboygan.
West Virginia.—J. M. Kirk, Wheeling.
Nebraska.—Prof. S. R. Thompson, Lincoln.
Tennessee.—Col. John Overton, Nashville.

New Jersey.—Dr. E. M. Hunt, Trenton.
Maryland.—Hon. John M. Robinson, Centreville.
District of Columbia.—Dr. D. E. Salmon, Washington.
Massachusetts.—Levi Stockbridge, Amherst.
Michigan.—Hon. William Ball, Hamburg.

Mr. STURGIS, of Wyoming. I wish to offer a resolution in connection with this committee that has been appointed. It is that a secretary be appointed from a central point in the West who shall correspond with the members of the committee selected to go to Washington, shall ascertain what numbers will actually go, shall communicate with each of those members who are to be their associates, and by appointing a fixed day for their meeting in Washington, thus insure unanimity of action. He shall provide the chairman with proper credentials and obtain proxies if originals cannot go. I move the adoption of the resolution.

The motion was agreed to.

Mr. STURGIS. I now nominate, with the consent of the Chair, the Hon. J. B. Grinnell as said secretary.

Professor MORROW, of Illinois. We all know Mr. Grinnell, and are all glad to have him upon this committee; but I am reminded that Mr. Grinnell is getting to be somewhat of an old man, and as the labor attaching to this office will be considerable I would suggest, without any consultation with him, the Hon. D. W. Smith, of Illinois. Of course if Mr. Grinnell will serve we should be glad to have him.

Mr. GOSPER, of Arizona. I understand that the secretary has such an assurance.

Mr. STURGIS, of Wyoming. I, of course, consulted some one before I took the liberty of proposing his name, and I was assured that he would throw himself into it, and do it with pleasure.

The nomination was agreed to unanimously.

Mr. CHORN, of Kentucky. I have a resolution which has been handed to the committee on resolutions, which I send to the secretary to be read.

The secretary read the resolution. It appears hereafter.

Mr. THOMPSON, of Nebraska. I will say that the resolution was handed me as a member of the committee on resolutions. The design is to call the attention of the States to this important subject and to call their attention to their specific duty, and it contemplates that this shall be done through the committee of this body appointed to confer with Congress on a similar subject.

The PRESIDENT. Won't you amend that to read " several States or the executive authorities of the same ? "

Mr. THOMPSON, of Nebraska. I move that those words be inserted.

The motion was agreed to, and the resolution, as amended, was adopted. It is as follows :

Whereas it is the duty of State legislatures to take measures to protect the owners of domestic animals from loss arising from the importation and spread of contagious diseases,

Be it resolved, That the committee of this Convention memorialize the legislatures of the several States, or the executive authorities of the same, urging upon them the importance of establishing a veterinary or health department for the prevention and spread of all such contagious diseases.

Mr. W. T. SMITH, of Iowa. We have had some very valuable articles read here upon the subject which was the cause of our convening. O course the all-important object is to prevent the spread of this great disease among us. It seems to me that anything we do to educate our people as to what the disease is, its great danger, and how to prevent it, how it may be carried, &c., is an important branch of our business I don't know what arrangements have been or are being made for the publication of these articles, but it seems to me it is an important part of our proceedings, and I have brought the subject before the Convention for the purpose of ascertaining if there have been any arrangements made by which they are to be published for the benefit of the public. If not we should make some arrangement before we adjourn. I don't know whether the live-stock journals have been represented here and have taken the proceedings with a view to their publication or not. If so, that will probably be sufficient.

The PRESIDENT. Dr. Loring has had here during our sessions his stenographer, who has taken a full report of the proceedings, and I understand it is his intention to publish them from his Department.

Dr. SALMON. As the representative of the Department of Agriculture here to-day, I wish to say that Dr. Loring has expressed his intention of publishing the full proceedings of this Convention, together with the papers that have been read.

It was agreed that the committee on legislation should meet at 7 p. m.

Mr. CAREY, of Wyoming. Mr. President, I am not as sanguine about legislation as some others of the committee. I fear there are many members of it who think that all they will have to do will be to go to Washington and ask Congressmen to legislate for us. I know how very difficult it is to get a bill through both branches of Congress even when very favorable circumstances surround it. I think that Commissioner Loring did a very wise thing indeed when he called a Stock Convention to meet at this time and place. Now almost every other industry has a permanent organization to consider that which affects their every interest. I therefore make this motion : That the president and secretary, or either of them, shall be authorized to call a convention of men representing the stock interests, to meet in this city next year at a suitable time during the progress of the Fat-Stock show, in order that we may hear and receive the report of the delegation we are sending to Washington, so that we gentlemen who have this matter so much at heart may know what is being done and what more is necessary to be done. The stock-growers of Wyoming issued a circular to the agricultural societies throughout the United States requesting them to send delegations to meet in this city and hold a convention during the time of this Fat-Stock show. The reason for our intense interest in this matter is not far to seek. We have men in that country who are importing from Europe; men who are producing the meat for this very market. We all know very well that if any contagious disease is introduced on the plains our business is surely ruined, and all the capital invested in that country will as surely pass out of existence. As an illustration of our watchfulness and of our dangers, and as showing the importance of this subject to us, one of our stock-growers went to Kentucky and bought, I think, 40 head. He unfortunately stopped those bulls in Saint Louis. They were met on the road by our authorized inspector, and the result was that those bulls were placed in quarantine, and I think 14 of them died. With regard to what my friend from Iowa (Mr. W. T. Smith) has said, I will state that, while we all acknowledge the importance and position of the cattle interest of Iowa, while we have no doubt that it is much larger than in any Territory, yet there is one fact in relation to the industry of Wyoming that must not be lost sight of, and in which it exceeds any State or Territory in the Union. The stock-raisers of our Territory went to the two States of Missouri and Iowa during the spring months of the present year to expend one million and a half of dollars in young cattle. Now for this we want absolute protection, so far as it is possible, from any contact with disease by shipping your cattle out there. We want the risk entirely removed, and we ask these more Eastern States who have Congressmen to come to us in our need. We have no Congressman; only a delegate. Our hundred millions of dollars has really no power or influence, we may say, in the city of Washington. The men who have votes there are the men who can trade votes, and are those who can influence legislation. A Congressman who has a pet measure can go to another who has a pet measure, and they can trade and log-roll and secure the legislation. The Territories are put off always to the last, and they only get the crumbs that fall from the table in the distribution of the money. [Applause.] Our business for 100 days preceding the first of November enabled us to place upon the Chicago market a thousand beeves each day. Let us remember that this mighty development has come almost entirely from the business which has grown up there since General Crook took possession of the country occupied by roving, worthless bands of Indians, and remembering it let us believe that those States where we are expending our money can well afford to take hold of this matter and furnish us, so far as possible, with protection from those diseases which already exist in the East. [Applause.] Now I desire to say further in behalf of our young Territory—the youngest of all of them—while we have built up this great industry, which is tributary almost entirely to this great State, we have not been negligent in enacting the necessary legislation. Be it said to the credit of Mr. Sturgis, who occupies a position here, and to Mr. Swan and Mr. Irving, that they have labored until they effected the passage of what we believe to be the best law ever passed on this subject. We have a salaried officer, an officer who has been very useful, and who has accomplished great good. We pay him, not a very large salary but as much as is paid to any officers sent there by the United States. But the stock-men had to make this compromise: they agreed to come forward as men and furnish the requisite money for the indemnity fund. In other words, all animals destroyed on account of disease are paid for by a direct tax on the stock interests. They go before the legislature, which meets early in January, and advocate appropriations all of which shall be levied on this business.

Mr. Sturgis has vouched for the association, of which he has so long been secretary, that that association would pay the expenses of its delegates. We ask no contribution. We only ask that every member of this committee be present in Washington, in season and out of season, if necessary; to go there this winter and to stay there urging this matter upon Congress until the dog-days, if need be, in order to accomplish what is of so vast importance to these Western States and Territories. [Applause.] We have taken hold of this matter in advance. We have not had a case of pleuro-pneumonia in Wyoming so far as we know. Our men there who have bought cattle as far east as New York, especially those men who, like Mr. Swan, make large importations from Great Britain, want protection from this disease. You will find that the sentiment is unanimous among our stock-raisers, and we believe that this is the sentiment of those men who stand at the head of the stock-growing interests of the United States. Now we believe we do not ask anything unreasonable when we request this committee to do all in its power to get for us what almost every other interest in the United States gets—a certain amount of protection at the hands of Congress. The Territory asks for protection, and we shall ask Congress for it, and we trust we shall get it, if we knock until they answer us. [Applause.]

After a remark of a delegate to which Mr. Carey replied, and which was more or less personal in its nature, a delegate said:

A DELEGATE. I produce cattle in Iowa for the purpose of making fine beef, and fine men, and making men feel happy. Now, if we have any disease that passes through Iowa, going west to the plains, we cannot be secure in these results. I believe that one case across the Missouri River will wipe out $500,000,000. I believe that no atmospheric influences, no locality, no geographical position, nor heat, nor cold, nor degree of latitude will exterminate pleuro-pneumonia, as I have heard some gentleman say.

The motion of Mr. Carey was then agreed to.

MR. CLAY, of Illinois. I would like to move a vote of thanks to our chairman, who has so ably conducted the business of this meeting. It has been, I know, a gratification that the State of Kentucky, which I, as a stockman, look upon as one of our great stock-producing States, should send us our chairman. The labors of General Williams in behalf of our cattle interest are well known to us all, and I only hope that he will live long after this country has become clear of pleuro-pneumonia, and every other disease to which the animal kingdom is subject. There are very few who have had more experience in the stock business than I. This is a great question and this Convention has handled it well. I hope the interest you have all manifested here will not die out, and that every stockman in this country will assist you in your efforts to the best of his ability.

The motion was unanimously agreed to.

A DELEGATE. The thought suggested itself to me after the motion made by my friend from Wyoming [Mr. Carey] with reference to the calling of another convention, that it might be a wise thing to set on foot a movement for the purpose of organizing a permanent national stock association. We meet now of course simply at the call of Commissioner Loring, and next year may be called together by our president and secretary, but will it be a permanent organization?

A DELEGATE. I move that the committee on legislation be requested carefully to consider the question of a permanent organization and that it, jointly with the president and secretary in due time, call a convention of delegates to complete a permanent organization, about one year from this time.

A DELEGATE. While that may accomplish the object, it occurs to me that if we divide the duties of that committee the one great duty for which they were appointed may be neglected. It appears to me that it would be better if in the call to be made by the present president and secretary they announce the object, as they do in any call for similar organizations.

A DELEGATE. I move that a vote of thanks be tendered to the secretary for the able manner in which he has discharged his duties.

The motion was unanimously agreed to.

A motion of thanks to the press was also adopted.

Mr. W. T. SMITH, of Iowa. In your opening address, your honor took occasion to show the necessity for having money to pay the way of those who are to seek this legislation. It seems to me that one of the most important things for us to consider is how we can furnish this means of subsistence, and for carrying out legislation. I suggest that this should be considered.

The PRESIDENT. I should suppose that each State would pay the expenses of its own delegate.

Mr. SMITH. I don't propose to make any motion of that kind, but let us have an understanding about it. Let it be understood that each State and Territory is to defray its own expenses. There is to some extent a little injustice in that perhaps, but I presume it would not be proper or necessary that we pass a resolution of that kind, but let us understand it.

Mr. THOMPSON, of Nebraska. I trust that every member of this Convention who is here now, or who has been here will consider himself a committee of one to write to every member of Congress he knows, and urge upon him the importance of this matter. It will have a great effect in securing the help we need. I have seen the effect of these personal appeals, and I know that they are valuable.

The PRESIDENT. The Secretary will read a letter which has been placed in his hands, and which explains itself.

The Secretary read the following letter:

CHICAGO, ILL., *November* 15, 1883.

GENTLEMEN: I am instructed by the board of management of the World's Industrial and Cotton Centennial Exposition to invite your association to hold its next annual meeting at New Orleans, La., upon the occasion of the opening of the World's Exposition on the first Monday of December, 1884. Efforts are being made to secure the attendance of stock breeders from all parts of the world, and, whilst this exposition will be international in its character, it will specially exhibit the products of the soil, mines, and forests of the South, and of Mexico and Central America. The people of the section primarily interested in the inventions and labor-saving machinery of this age of progress are no less deeply interested in improving their breeds of horses, cattle, hogs, sheep, and poultry, and questions relating thereto. The holding of your convention at the opening of this World's Exposition would enlarge the scope of your labors, and in benefiting the section of country referred to would no doubt promote the objects you have in view.

I am, very respectfully,

C. A. BURKE,
Director-General.

PRESIDENT AND MEMBERS NATIONAL STOCK CONVENTION,
Chicago, Ills.

A DELEGATE. I move that a vote of thanks be tendered for this invitation.

The motion was agreed to.

Mr. CHORN, of Kentucky. I now move that we adjourn *sine die.*

The president (after putting the motion). The motion is agreed to, and this Convention stands adjourned without day. [Applause.]

INDEX.

	Page.

Alabama:
    Delegate enrolled 4
Alwood, William:
    Accredited as a delegate from Ohio................................. 5
Amendments proposed to:
    Report of committee on resolutions 58, 61, 65, 66
Anderson, T. C.:
    Accredited as a delegate from Kentucky............................. 4
    Appointed on committee on legislation............................. 68
Arizona:
    Delegate enrolled 4
Baker, Aaron:
    Accredited as a delegate from West Virginia 5
Baldwin, L. C.:
    Accredited as a delegate from Iowa................................ 4
Ball, William:
    Accredited as a delegate from Michigan............................ 4
    Appointed on committee on legislation............................. 69
Bartlett, ——, Illinois.:
    Remarks by, on calf trade... 42
Bath, Obed:
    Accredited as a delegate from West Virginia....................... 5
Batters, Hon. Alfred, of Colorado.:
    Elected a vice-president of Convention............................. 13
Bean, A. C.:
    Accredited as a delegate from Kentucky 4
Beatty, Prof. Simon:
    Delegate from Province of Ontario, admitted........................ 6
Bonham, L. N.:
    Accredited as a delegate from Ohio 5
    Appointed on committee on resolutions 32
Bonnett, D.:
    Accredited as a delegate from Iowa................................ 4
Brayton, W. C.:
    Accredited as a delegate from New York 5
Brigham, J. H.:
    Accredited as a delegate from Ohio 5
Brockway, E. F.:
    Accredited as a delegate from Iowa 4
Brown, J. D.:
    Accredited as a delegate from Iowa 4
Buchanan, T. H.:
    Accredited as a delegate from West Virginia....................... 5
Burke, C. A.:
    Letter from, inviting delegates to hold next Convention in New Orleans .. 74
    Resolution of thanks for same..................................... 74
Butterfield, jr., I. H.:
    Accredited as a delegate from Michigan............................ 4
    Appointed on committee on permanent organization.................. 6
    Appointed on committee on resolutions............................. 57
Calf trade:
    Remarks on, by several members................................... 41–43
Canada:
    Delegates from, admitted.. 6
Carey, Hon. J. M.:
    Accredited as a delegate from Wyoming............................. 5
    Appointed on committee on legislation............................. 68
    Appointed on committee on permanent organization.................. 6
    Appointed on committee on resolutions 56
    General remarks by.. 68

Page.

Carey, Hon. J. M.:
Motion by, authorizing the calling of a future convention 70
Motion adopted 72
Motion to amend 30
Remarks by, on motion to adjourn 30
Remarks by, concerning legislation and cattle interest in Wyoming 70
Carnss, R. B.:
Accredited as a delegate from Michigan 4
Carskaden, I. P.:
Accredited as a delegate from West Virginia 5
Carskaden, T. R.:
Accredited as a delegate from West Virginia 5
Appointed on committee on permanent organization 6
Case, George E.:
Accredited as a delegate from Minnesota 4
Appointed on committee on resolutions 57
Chairman (temporary) chosen 5
Chamberlain, W. I.:
Accredited as a delegate from Ohio 5
Appointed on committee on order of business 9
Presents report of committee on order of business 17
Chambers, J. M.:
Accredited as a delegate from Illinois.... 4
Chase, George:
Accredited as a delegate from Iowa 4
Chorn, James:
Accredited as a delegate from Kentucky.................................. 4
Appointed on committee on permanent organization...................... 6
Appointed on committee on resolutions 32
Incidental remarks by..................................... .... 30, 31
Motion by.. 30
Motion by, to adjourn sine die adopted 74
Presents report of committee on resolutions. 57
Reports resolution relative to co-operation of State legislatures......... 69
Circular:
Call for Convention 3
Clark, J.:
Accredited as a delegate from Iowa 4
Remarks by, on prevalence of cattle disease............................ 12, 13
Clark, J. H.:
Accredited as delegate from Pennsylvania............................... 5
Clay, John:
Accredited as a delegate from Wyoming.................................. 5
Motion by, expressing thanks to president of Convention 73
Cochran, Hon. M. H.:
Delegate from Province of Quebec, admitted............................. 6
Elected a vice-president of Convention................................ 13
Cockrill, M. S.:
Accredited as a delegate from Tennessee 5
Coffin, L. S.:
Accredited as a delegate from Iowa..................................... 4
Elected temporary secretary.. 5
Incidental remarks by.. 52, 66
Paper by 52
Remarks by... 16
Remarks by, on prevalence of cattle disease............................ 12
Colorado:
Delegates enrolled 4
Committee on legislation:
Appointed 63
Remarks by delegates relative to expenses of.......................... 73
Committee on order of business:
Appointed 9
Reports... 17
Further report adopted.. 44
Submits further report 37
Committee on permanent organization:
Appointed 5
Report.. 13

Page.

Committee on resolutions:
  Appointed 31
  Membership of, increased 57
  Membership of, increased to one delegate from each State and Territory... 57
  Presents report 57
  Amendments proposed thereto....................................58, 61, 65. 66
  Report of first section agreed to 58
  First section amended.. 61
  First resolution stricken out.. 63
  Second resolution adopted as reported 65
  Third resolution adopted as amended.. 66
  Fourth resolution adopted as reported 66
  Report of, as amended and adopted 67
Convention:
  Call for... 3
  Called to order by Professor Morrow 3
Corwin, J.:
  Accredited as a delegate from Ohio... 5
Cotton, Prof. T. B.:
  Accredited as a delegate from Ohio 5
Cowden, W. N.:
  Accredited as a delegate from Ohio 5
  Appointed on committee on permanent organization 6
Crane, John:
  Accredited as a delegate from New Jersey..................................... 5
  Remarks by, on disease of cattle in New Jersey 47
  Incidental remarks by.. 49
Culbertson, C. M.:
  Accredited as a delegate from Illinois....................................... 4
Culver, Carey:
  Accredited as a delegate from Colorado....................................... 4
Culver, ——:
  Accredited as a delegate from Colorado 4
Curtis, Col. F. D.:
  Accredited as a delegate from New York 4
Curtis, G. W.:
  Accredited as a delegate from Illinois.......................................
Curtis, Col. N. M.:
  Appointed on committee on legislation 68
Dailey, William:
  Accredited as a delegate from Nebraska....................................... 5
  Presents name of S. R. Thompson as a member of committee on resolutions 57
Delano, Hon. Columbus:
  Appointed on committee on legislation.. 68
Delatast, W. S.:
  Accredited as a delegate from Ohio 5
Delegates:
  List of.. 1–5
Delegates:
  Motions by... 6, 31
Delegate:
  Motion by, to limit debate, agreed to.. 58
Delegates:
  Remarks by various...16, 52, 54, 72
Delegate, a:
  Remarks by, concerning a permanent organization 73
  Suggests plan of action for Convention....................................... 55
Detmers, Dr. H. J.:
  Remarks by, on motion to strike out first resolution reported by committee
    on resolutions 62
Dick, Governor:
  Appointed on committee on resolutions 57
Dinsmore, W. M.:
  Accredited as a delegate from Pennsylvania................................... 5
District of Columbia:
  Delegate enrolled 4
Dodge, Calvin:
  Accredited delegate from Ohio.. 5

Page.

Donse, O. M.:
  Accredited as a delegate from Nebraska.......................   5
Dunn, John:
  British vice-consul, invited to seat in Convention by general consent......   10
Dwin, M. L.:
  Accredited as a delegate from Iowa   4
Emory, Edward B.:
  Accredited as a delegate from Maryland   4
  Appointed on committee on permanent organization   6
  Appointed on committee on resolutions   57
  Elected an assistant secretary of Convention   13
  Remarks by, on motion to amend report of committee on resolutions   58
  Remarks by, relative to pleuro-pneumonia in Maryland   59–60
Estell, W.W.:
  Accredited as a delegate from Kentucky   4
Estell, C.:
  Accredited as a delegate from Kentucky   4
Esten, C. R.:
  Accredited as a delegate from Kentucky   4
Expenses of committee on legislation:
  Remarks and suggestions relative thereto by various members   73–74
Fergus, Samuel P.:
  Accredited as a delegate from Pennsylvania.........................   5
Fleming, Frank:
  Accredited as a delegate from Ohio   5
Fleming, James W.:
  Accredited as a delegate from Ohio   5
Foster, D. N.:
  Accredited as a delegate from Illinois...............................   4
Foster, W. S.:
  Accredited as a delegate from Ohio   5
Gadsden, Prof. John W..
  Accredited as a delegate from Pennsylvania   5
  Paper by..   49
  Remarks by..47, 48, 49
  Remarks by, on motion to amend report of committee on resolutions......   59
  Remarks by, on prevalence of cattle disease...........................   13
  Remarks by, on motion to strike out first resolution reported by committee
    on resolutions...   63
Garner, W.:
  Accredited as a delegate from Kentucky   4
Gay, D. A.:
  Accredited as a delegate from Kentucky   4
Goldschmidt, May:
  Accredited as a delegate from Wyoming.................................   5
Gould, John:
  Accredited as a delegate from Ohio   5
Gosper, J. G.:
  Accredited as a delegate from Arizona   4
  Appointed on committee on legislation.................................   68
  Appointed on committee on resolutions   57
  Motion by, to appoint Mr. Sturgis temporary secretary...................   5
  Remarks by...   16, 68
Grange, Prof. E. A. A.:
  Accredited as a delegate from Michigan...............................   4
Griffin, H. B.:
  Accredited as a delegate from Iowa...................................   4
Grinnell, Hon. J. B.:
  Accredited as a delegate from Iowa...................................   4
  Appointed on committee on legislation.................................   67
  Appointed secretary of committee on legislation...................   69
  Motion by, to adopt first portion of report of committee on resolutions.... 57
  Motion by, to amend third resolution of report of committee on resolutions. 65
  Amendment adopted   66
  Motion by, to limit each speaker...   19
  Remarks by, on animal diseases...   9
  Remarks by, on motion to strike out first resolution reported by committee
    on resolutions...   62
Hamilton, A. W.:
  Accredited as a delegate from Kentucky   4

Hamilton, George:
　　Accredited as a delegate from Kentucky 4
Hamilton, Governor:
　　Address of welcome 7
Hamilton, J. C.:
　　Accredited as a delegate from Kentucky................... 4
Hamilton, W. W.:
　　Accredited as a delegate from Kentucky...... 4
Hardin, S. H.:
　　Accredited as a delegate from Wyoming 5
Harris, Joseph:
　　Accredited as a delegate from New York................................ 5
Harris, L. B.:
　　Accredited as a delegate from Ohio ....,..... 5
Henderson, James L.:
　　Accredited as a delegate from Pennsylvania 5
Henry, Prof. M. A.:
　　Accredited as a delegate from Wisconsin................................ 5
Hill, G.:
　　Accredited as a delegate from Kentucky 4
Holden, G.:
　　Accredited as a delegate from Wyoming 5
Hopkins, Prof. James D.:
　　Accredited as a delegate from Wyoming 5
　　Paper by, on means of exterminating contagious diseases among animals.. 44
　　Remarks by, on motion to amend report of committee on resolutions....58, 59, 60
　　Remarks by, on motion to strike out first resolution reported by committee
　　　　on resolutions.. 62
　　Remarks by, on motion to amend third resolution of report of committee
　　　　on resolutions.. 66
　　Remarks by, on report of committee on resolutions....................... 57
Hostetter, A. B.:
　　Accredited as a delegate from Illinois................................... 4
Howell, C.:
　　Accredited as a delegate from Kentucky 4
Huidekoper, Edgar:
　　Accredited as a delegate from Pennsylvania 5
Hunt, Dr. E. M.:
　　Appointed on committee on legislation 69
Hunton, John:
　　Accredited as a delegate from Wyoming 5
Illinois:
　　Delegate enrolled 4
Introduction:
　　Of Governor Hamilton 7
Invitation:
　　To hold next convention in New Orleans, La........ 74
Iowa:
　　Delegates enrolled 4
Irvine, Hon. W. C.:
　　Accredited as a delegate from Wyoming 5
Johnson, W. P.:
　　Accredited as a delegate from Tennessee ....
Kellogg, R. D.:
　　Accredited as a delegate from Iowa.................................... 4
　　Remarks by, on prevalence of cattle disease 10, 11
Kendall, J.:
　　Accredited as a delegate from Kentucky............................... 4
Kentucky:
　　Delegates from, enrolled.. 4
Kirk, J. M.:
　　Accredited as a delegate from West Virginia............................ 5
　　Appointed on committee on legislation 69
　　Appointed on committee on resolutions................................ 57
Kirk, O. M.:
　　Accredited as a delegate from West Virginia............................ 5
Law, Prof. James:
　　Accredited as a delegate from New York 4
　　Appointed on committee on permanent organization...... 6

                                                                          Page.
Law, Prof. James:
    Incidental remarks by 49
    Introduced to convention... 19
    Motion to strike out first resolution from report of committee on resolu-
        tions.. 61
    Remarks by, on 63
    Motion agreed to... 63
    Paper by... 19
    Incidental remarks by.. 54
    Remarks by, on adoption of second resolution, reported by committee on
        resolutions.. 64
    Remarks by, on calf trade and cattle disease....................... 43
    Remarks by, relative to pleuro-pneumonia in Maryland............... 59
    Remarks by, relative to Treasury quarantine at Philadelphia........ 52
Lawrence, M. J.:
    Accredited as a delegate from Ohio   5
    Incidental remarks by.. 40, 41
    Remarks on report of committee on order of business................ 18
Le Moyne, Julius:
    Accredited as a delegate from Pennsylvania.........................   5
    Appointed on committee on legislation.............................. 68
    Appointed on committee on resolutions 57
Lemnust, —— :
    Accredited as a delegate from Ohio   5
Levering, J. C.:
    Accredited as a delegate from Ohio   5
Lewis, O. A.:
    Accredited as a delegate from West Virginia   5
Loving, George B.:
    Accredited as a delegate from Texas................................   5
    Appointed on committee on legislation.............................. 68
Maryland:
    Delegate from, enrolled   4
Massachusetts:
    Delegate from, enrolled   4
Matthew, W. R.:
    Accredited as a delegate from Iowa   4
McFarland, J. D.:
    Accredited as a delegate from Alabama..............................   4
    Appointed on committee on permanent organization..................   6
McKerrnan, W. B.:
    Accredited as a delegate from Pennsylvania.........................   5
McMurtrie, Prof. William:
    Remarks during preliminary proceedings.............................   4
Metcalf, H. J.:
    Accredited as a delegate from Colorado   4
Maxwell, —— :
    Accredited as a delegate from Colorado.............................   4
Michigan:
    Delegates from, enrolled...   4
Miller, G. S.:
    Accredited as a delegate from New York   5
Minnesota:
    Delegates from, enrolled...   4
Moninger, D. M.:
    Accredited as a delegate from Iowa   4
Moore, C. T.:
    Accredited as a delegate from Michigan.............................   4
Morgan, George:
    Accredited as a delegate from Wyoming..............................   5
Morgan, James:
    Accredited as a delegate from Iowa.................................   4
Morrow, Prof. G. E.:
    Accredited as a delegate from Illinois   4
    Announces presence of Mr. Dunn, vice-consul of Great Britain....... 10
    Elected temporary chairman, and remarks by   5
    Elected a vice-president of Convention 13
    Incidental remarks by.. 5, 6, 9
    Introduces Governor Hamilton   7
    Introduces permanent president to Convention....................... 13

Morrow, Prof. G. E.:
    Nominates Hon. D. W. Smith to be secretary of committee on resolutions ..   69
    Remarks by, on motion to amend report of committee on resolutions   59
    Remarks upon calling Convention to order..............................   3
    Incidental remarks by...   95
Murray, A. J.:
    Accredited as a delegate from Michigan................................   4
    Appointed on committee of order of business...........................   9
Nebraska:
    Delegates from, enrolled   5
New Jersey:
    Delegates from, enrolled   5
    Statement relative to, by Mr. Crane   47
    Statement relative to, by Dr. Gadsden.................................   48
Newton, Prof. I. V.:
    Accredited as a delegate from Ohio   5
New York:
    Delegates from, enrolled   4-5
Niles, O. E.:
    Accredited as a delegate from Ohio   5
Niles, Professor:
    Accredited as a delegate from Ohio   5
Nugent, W. R.:
    Accredited as a delegate from Iowa   4
Officers:
    Permanent, elected   13
    Temporary, elected   5-6
Ohio:
    Delegates from, enrolled..   5
Order of business:
    Committee on, further report adopted..................................   44
    Committee on, submits further report..................................   37
Organization:
    Report of committee on permanent   13
Overton, John:
    Accredited as a delegate from Tennessee   5
    Appointed on committee on legislation   68
    Appointed on committee on resolutions   57
Owen, R.:
    Accredited as a delegate from Kentucky................................   4
Papers presented:
    By Prof. James Law, of New York......................................   19
    By Dr. D. E. Salmon, of the United States Department of Agriculture   32
    By Prof. J. D. Hopkins, of Wyoming   44
    By Prof. John W. Gadsden, of Pennsylvania   49
    By Hon. L. S. Coffin, of Iowa...   52
Parker, W. H.:
    Accredited as a delegate from Wyoming   5
Parsons, W. R.:
    Accredited as a delegate from Ohio   5
Parsons, P.:
    Remarks by, on prevalence of cattle disease...........................   11
Paxton, J. G.:
    Accredited as a delegate from Pennsylvania............................   5
Pennsylvania:
    Delegates from, enrolled..   5
    Statement relative to disease in, by Dr. Gadsden   51
Phelps, Edwin:
    Accredited as a delegate from Michigan................................   4
Phillips, E. R.:
    Accredited as a delegate from Michigan................................   4
Pickrell, J. H.:
    Accredited as a delegate from Illinois................................   4
    Appointed on committee on order of business   9
Pickrell, Watson:
    Accredited as a delegate from Nebraska................................   5
Points, W.:
    Accredited as a delegate from Kentucky   4
Post, Mr.:
    Remarks by   56

Page.

Powell, E. A.:
  Accredited as a delegate from New York 5
  Elected a vice-president of Convention........ 13
Pratt, J. H.:
  Accredited as a delegate from Wyoming... 5
Prentice, Professor, of Illinois:
  Remarks by.. 11, 12
President:
  Of Convention, elected.. 13
  Incidental remarks by 52
  Remarks by, on report of committee on order of business.................. 18
President (pro tempore):
  Remarks by... 30–37
  Suggests appointment of committee on resolutions........................... 31
Reconsideration:
  Of vote adopting third resolution, reported by committee on resolutions... 66
Redfield, Mr :
  Appointed on committee on resolutions 32
Remick, R. A.:
  Accredited as a delegate from Michigan.................................... 4
Report:
  Of committee on order of business, adopted.................................. 37
  Of committee on order of business, read and adopted 17–19
  Of committee on permanent organization 13
  Of committee on resolutions. First section agreed to..................... 58
Resolutions:
  Committee on, increased... 57
  Committee on, presents report.. 57
  Committee on, first section of report agreed to............................ 58
  Committee on, second resolution adopted.................................... 65
  Committee on, third resolution adopted as amended 66
  Committee on, fourth resolution adopted as reported...................... 66
  Committee on, motion to reconsider adoption of third resolution ageed to. 66
  Committee on, report amended 61
  First resolution in report of committee on, stricken out 63
  Committee on, report adopted as amended.................................... 67
  Relative to co-operation of State legislature, amended and adopted 70
  Of thanks to Mr. Sturgis, secretary of Convention 73
  Of thanks to press.. 73
  Of thanks voted to Hon. John S. Williams, the president................. 73
  Of thanks to C. A. Burke.. 74
Roberts, Prof. J. P.:
  Accredited as a delegate from New York.. 5
  Motion by, to appoint committee on resolutions 31
  Incidental remarks by.. 31
  Motion to amend report of Committee on Resolutions and remarks thereon. 58, 59
  Motion agreed to.. 61
Robinson, I. S.:
  Accredited as a delegate from Ohio 5
Robinson, Hon John M.:
  Appointed on committee on legislation 69
Roll call of States and Territories 4
Rusk, G. W.:
  Accredited as delegate from Colorado 4
  Appointed on committee on resolutions.. 57
Salmon, Dr. D. E.:
  Accredited as delegate representing United States Department of Agriculture 4
  Appointed on committee on legislation 69
  Appointed on committee on permanent organization....................... 6
  Appointed on committee on resolutions 57
  Reads paper on prevention of contagious diseases in America 32
  Remarks by, concerning publication of proceedings by the Department of Agriculture 70
Sanders, J. H.:
  Accredited as a delegate from Illinois.. 4
  Address to Convention 37
  Appointed on committee on resolutions 32
  Incidental remarks by 66

Page.

Sanders, J. H. :
  Motion by, to adopt report of committee on resolutions 57
  Remarks during preliminary proceedings 4
  Remarks upon hour of meetings 7
  Remarks by, on courtesies to Mr. Dunn 10
  Remarks by, on adoption of second resolution reported by committee on
    resolutions 64
  Remarks by, on calf trade 42
  Remarks by, on motion to strike out first resolution reported by committee
    on resolutions 61–63
Scott, C. :
  Accredited as a delegate from Kentucky 4
Scott, Hon. John :
  Accredited as a delegate from Iowa 4
  Appointed on committee on resolutions 57
  Remarks by, and motion to increase membership of committee on resolu-
    tions 56
  Remarks by, on motion to strike out first resolution reported by committee
    on resolutions 62
  Remarks by 54
Scott, J. R. :
  Accredited as a delegate from Illinois 4
  Appointed on committee on permanent organization 6
Secretaries:
  Elected 13
Secretary (temporary):
  Elected 5
Shafer, J. R. :
  Accredited as a delegate from Iowa 4
Shaver, J. K. :
  Accredited as a delegate from Illinois 4
Shook, Z. E. :
  Accredited as a delegate from Ohio 5
Sisson, L. P. :
  Accredited as a delegate from West Virginia 5
Skinner, R. C. :
  Accredited as a delegate from Ohio 5
Smith, Carey R. :
  Accredited as a delegate from Iowa 4
  Appointed on committee on order of business 9
  Motion by, to appoint committee on order of business 9
  Remarks by, on 9
  Presents report of committee on permanent organization 13
  Submits further report of committee on order of business 44
  Submits further report from committee on order of business 37
  Remarks by, on report of committee on order of business 18
Smith, D. W. :
  Accredited as a delegate from Illinois 4
  Appointed on committee on legislation 68
  Nominated to be secretary of committee on legislation 69
Smith, Hon. Hiram :
  Accredited as a delegate from Wisconsin 5
  Appointed on committee on legislation 68
  Appointed on committee on permanent organization 6
  Appointed on committee on resolutions 57
Smith, W. T. :
  Accredited as a delegate from Iowa 4
  Appointed as acting chairman of committee on permanent organization ... 6
  Appointed on committee on permanent organization 6
  Appointed on committee on resolutions 32
  Remarks by, on calf trade 41–43
  Remarks by, concerning expenses of committee on legislation 73
  Remarks by, concerning publication of proceedings 70
  Nominates Hon. J. B. Grinnell as a member of committee on legislation 67
  Remarks by, on motion to amend report of committee on resolutions 60
  Incidental remarks by 68
Snouffer, J. J. :
  Accredited as a delegate from Iowa 4

Page.

Sproat, Joseph :
Accredited as a delegate from Iowa.. 4
Stacey, Fitch B. :
Accredited as a delegate from Iowa.. 4
States and Territories :
Roll called................. 4
Steddon, M. P. :
Accredited as a delegate from Ohio............ 5
Stevens, —— :
Accredited as a delegate from Wyoming 5
Stockbridge, Levi (Massachusetts) :
Appointed on committee on legislation.................................... 69
Sturgis, Hon. Thomas :
Accredited as a delegate from Wyoming.................................... 5
Address to convention... 16
Declines nomination for temporary secretary............................ 5
Elected secretary of Convention 13
Incidental remarks by.. 69
Motion by, to appoint secretary of committee on legislation adopted 69
Nominates Professor Morrow as temporary chairman 5
Remarks by, on appointment committee on order of business 9
Remarks by, on third resolution of report of committee on resolutions..... 66
Swan, Hon. A. H. :
Accredited as a delegate from Wyoming 5
Sweet, ——.
Accredited as a delegate from Michigan.................................. 4
Taylor, B. H.
Accredited as a delegate from Iowa 4
Temporary chairman chosen.. 5
Temporary secretary chosen.. 5
Tennessee :
Delegates from, enrolled.. 5
Teschemacher, Hon. H. E. :
Accredited as a delegate from Wyoming 5
Texas :
Delegates from, enrolled.. 5
Thayer, Prof. L. S. :
Accredited as a delegate from Massachusetts............................. 4
Appointed on committee on permanent organization....................... 6
Appointed on committee on resolutions 57
Thompson, C. :
Accredited as a delegate from Kentucky 4
Remarks by.. 6
Thompson, J. M. :
Accredited as a delegate from Illinois..................................... 4
Thompson, J. M.:
Accredited as a delegate from Pennsylvania............................. 5
Thompson, Prof. S. R. :
Accredited as a delegate from Nebraska 5
Appointed on committee on legislation 68
Appointed on committee on permanent organization...................... 6
Appointed on committee on resolutions 57
Remarks by, on calf trade... 43
Remarks by, on report of committee on resolutions..................... 57
Remarks by, on motion to strike out first resolution reported by committee
on resolutions.. 63
Remarks by, concerning resolution relative to co-operation of State legis-
latures 69
Thornton, J. C.:
Accredited as a delegate from Pennsylvania............................. 5
Appointed on committee on permanent organization...................... 6
Todd, D. W.:
Accredited as a delegate from Ohio 5
Todd, S. H.:
Accredited as a delegate from Ohio...................................... 5
Torrey, R. A.:
Accredited as a delegate from Wyoming 5
Tracy, B. A.:
Accredited as a delegate from Kentucky................................. 4

Page.

Van Meter, B. F.:
Accredited as a delegate from Kentucky.................................... 4
Appointed on committee on order of business............................. 9
Vice-Presidents elected.. 13
Wales, Thomas B.:
Accredited as a delegate from Iowa...................................... 4
Walker, P. G.:
Accredited as a delegate from Pennsylvania........................... 5
Ward, S. E.:
Accredited as a delegate from Missouri................................. 4
Appointed on committee on permanent organization................... 6
Waugh, C. P.:
Accredited as a delegate from West Virginia............................ 5
Wheeler, H. C.:
Accredited as a delegate from Iowa..................................... 4
Webb, R. C.:
Accredited as a delegate from Iowa..................................... 4
Weltz, Leo:
Accredited as a delegate from Ohio..................................... 5
West Virginia:
Delegates from, enrolled... 5
Wilcox, J. E.:
Accredited as a delegate from Tennessee............................... 5
Appointed on committee on permanent organization................... 6
Williams, Hon. J. S.:
Accredited as a delegate from Kentucky................................ 4
Address by, upon assuming the chair...................................... 13
Elected president of Convention 13
Introduced to Convention by Professor Morrow 13
Proposes amendment to resolution relative to co-operation of State legisla-
tures 69
Remarks by upon, hour of meeting 6
Remarks by, concerning publication of proceedings 70
Wilson, James B.:
Accredited as a delegate from Pennsylvania........................... 5
Wilson, W. J.:
Accredited as a delegate from Colorado 4
Appointed on committee on legislation................................... 68
Appointed on committee on permanent organization.................. 6
Wing, ——:
Accredited as a delegate from New York 5
Winslow, P.:
Accredited as a delegate from Nebraska................................ 5
Wisconsin:
Delegates from, enrolled... 5
Yarr, W.:
Accredited as a delegate from Kentucky................................ 4
Yeomans, T. G.:
Accredited as a delegate from New York 4
Remarks by.. 10

www.ingramcontent.com/pod-product-compliance
Lightning Source LLC
Chambersburg PA
CBHW020309090426
42735CB00009B/1287